Happiness
with
Success

Psychological Approach and Interpretations

PROF. P. RAMACHANDRA PODUVAL

(Former Professor and Director, School of Management Studies

&

Dean, Faculty of Social Sciences

Cochin University of Science and Technology)

ISBN
Paperback 979-8-89724-295-5
Hardcase 979-8-89777-300-8

Dedication

This book is to be dedicated to a person who possesses an exemplary personality. One such person in my personal experience is the late Professor V.V. John. He was a pioneer in the field of higher education and a former Vice Chancellor of Jodhpur University. Prof. John was a model personality in the professional and personal life who proved by his own life that a man of inner strength and purity can overcome all adversities in life. The message that he gave to me and others is: 'Sreyas' (Happiness with success) is far superior to 'Preyas' (success by possessions and positions)

Contents

Foreword

Sri. Ananthanarayanan S.

Pavilion apartments, P.T. Usha Road,

Kochi-682011.

We are holding in our hand the book 'Happiness with Success' by Prof. Ramachandra Poduval, a teacher who has seen a thousand full moons. I am very pleased to present to you the background and specialities of this book that provide more knowledge to those involved in the fields of psychology, management, and experts in employee selection and training.

All those who lead a society, an institution or a movement in life are desirous of success in their endeavours. Being able to enjoy happiness along with success is a desirable thing. When we talk about happiness, we mean the happiness of being united with all the participants of the endeavour without any selfishness.

The qualities required for this are not acquired by birth alone. Experts believe that it can be cultivated through training. Some scales are needed to measure the personal qualities before and after the training and some indices are required to analyze the results. All such studies are conducted by psychologists in their efforts at demystifying the intricacies of the mind.

Our body is gross and our mind is subtle. The body can be seen by the eyes and known by the touch. Gender, shape, colour, strength etc., can be measured by their respective measurements and similar things can be placed in separate categories. When people are selected for specific purposes, measurements are taken to ensure that the selection strictly adheres to the criteria set by the selectors. Such a selection process are easily understandable and are used by both the candidates and the selectors.

However, qualities such as intelligence, character, and behaviour (as far as we know) are based on the process going on in the brain and cannot be directly measured by our senses. All these together we call the 'qualities of the mind'. Since the psychological qualities required for an employee cannot be measured by a physical scale or a balance machine, many psychologists have invented other methods to select those who possess these qualities at a desirable level. These are called psychometric tests and are often used by companies for employee selections and higher education institutions for admissions to different courses. GMAT, GRE, CAT, etc., are such admission tests

The measurements of blood pressure, sugar contents in the blood, cholesterol etc, are some indications of physical health. If it is deficient or in excess, those who have studied health sciences know everything about the cause, remedies and other relevant information. They have made some rough standards as indicator of the health status (BP 120/80; Sugar 110/200). It is revised from time to time in the light of experience and is communicated to the public. And there is a department called pharmacy for the manufacture of medicines and also quality control boards. If some of the problems are known only to some experts, it is customary then, to refer to them for a solution.

There are many specialists in physiology. But, other than psychologists and psychiatrists, not many specialists are there in the field of mental health. Psychological measurements and the indices they provide are not as familiar to the layman as they are in physiology. (Except IQ and EQ). An aptitude test is the only psychometric test that one takes in one's life pursuing higher studies or an employment. Most people don't know on what basis such tests for measurements are created. Some of the tonics available in the book stores for increasing the scores in such tests are those of 'Robin Sharma' and 'Shiva Khera' style books that appear as personality development aids. The impacts of such aids have never been tested. There are many labs to test the physical and physiological status (which sprout like mushrooms) but none to test the status of the mind.

Professor Ramachandra Poduval, who has had a long and distinguished career in both academic and practical fields, sheds light on some of the unknown areas of these issues to understand them deeply. He introduces the readers to the great masters who wrote their theories on Personality. Some of them we have heard of, like Freud and Jung.

A disease-free body is called 'healthy' and an 'athletic body' toned by exercise and hard work is attractive and desirable. So is the mind. Although the aforementioned criteria are used by psychologists to diagnose whether a person has a mental illness or not, the athletic healthy aspect of mental health is emphasised by the Professor in the third chapter on 'Positive Psychology'. Certain studies in positive psychology are focussed on discovering and shaping minds that burn themselves like candles and brighten the lives of others. Like a professor in Anatomy teaching the parts of the body, the author highlights in this Chapter the faculties to be investigated in the interior of the mind. Not all of them work independently. The professor also reminds us that they are inherent. In the fourth chapter, the professor explains the psychometric scales developed by various experts to measure mental health. When looking at the results of the lab test, you would have noticed that it is indicated in small letters at the bottom of the result which method was used for the test. We do not go into its details. Moreover, the professor explains, it also would indicate what the score of these means, as you can analyze the health level by looking at its results. These, undoubtedly, seem to be very useful for research students.

The essence of the professor's Study is encapsulated in Chapter 5. In Chapter 5, the professor enumerates the personal attributes that one should have to be an efficient, successful and happy manager. Then the professor goes on in search of a single, simple, reliable test to measure these qualities in a person within a limited time – as an aid for the recruiting team to make a proper selection. Keeping the universally known 'Minnesota Multiphasic Personality Inventory' (MMPI) with 566 statements as the base, the professor distills it through several filters (including the cultural stability to Indian/Oriental ethos), to arrive at a manageable 92 statements for which response is sought. This is further divided into 12 subscales. Further, like an 'ayurveda' physician making a powerful concoction with a suitable combination of herbs, professor Poduval uses them to arrive at two factors, viz. a 'People oriented factor' and a 'Performance oriented factor'. Ultimately, he combines these two to arrive at a single value term 'personal efficacy' index. This exercise gave rise to a novel, reliable test called 'Poduval's Personal Efficacy Test' (PPET), a desi, simplified version of MMPI to help select a prospective manager in the making, who will bring happiness with success in the organization.

In the subsequent Chapters, The professor elaborates with reasons, the traits one should be looking for in a prospective manager-aspirant, who would achieve happiness with success. It includes assertiveness (as explained in Chapter 6), Social extroversion and leadership role in social groups (Chapter 7), adoption of the 'I am OK, You are OK' attitude (Chapter 8), ability to empathize or counsel plus communication capability (Chapter 9), and ability to be proactive and decisive (Chapter 10).

The reading of the above mentioned five chapters leaves us with a bouquet of ten traits which the professor further ensconcise into two cells: 'People orientation factor' and the 'Performance oriented factor'. These two can be combined into single trait as the 'personal efficacy' index, which will tell you whether you have hit up on a candidate who is a prospective manger who will reap 'Happiness with Success' as against a person who will pursue success alone. The professor rooted in the oriental ethos labels the former as one seeking 'Sreyas' and the latter as one in pursuit of the not so desirable 'Preyas'.

An alternative title for this book could have been 'In Search of a Manager with 'Sreyas', as the professor may agree. Without doubt, the glossary and references at the end of each chapter definitely elevates the reference value of this book.

Psychological research is not a very capital intensive field. We are yet to tap into its endless possibilities. Following the footsteps of Poduval sir, the young generation can find new psychometric scales that are suitable for us. Using new technologies such as artificial intelligence and pattern recognition, one can try measurement scales and graphical presentations to make mind quality measurements more quickly and accurately. My humble opinion is that psychiatry or clinical psychology should invent a 'mental training package', a procedure equivalent to surgery. One is hardware replacement and the other is software up-gradation. It would be a desirable act on the part of the authorities to include basic concepts and theories of psychology in the school and college curriculum. I feel that this book is a suitable source book for that purpose.

In Kerala, there is no great work-culture that we can boast of. As the head of a research institution in Kerala, I could create an environment conducive to organizational effectiveness with efficiency. I retired from service with happy feelings. This background is the only credential that prompted me to agree to write this foreword to this distinguished book. I take this opportunity to express my gratitude to my friend Dr. B.J. Meledam, who gave me the opportunity to express my views on the book.

Prof. Poduval has provided enough resources for assimilation by the researchers of psychology, those working in the human resource development departments, candidates for jobs and their selectors and those who want to achieve excellence in the field of management. No doubt, this book will be an asset to all libraries, especially those at the college and university levels.

A Different Reading Experience

Dr. B.J. Meledom

CEO, Synergy Systems, Kochi.

Professor Ramachandra Poduval is my mentor and teacher. I have read most of his books and writing a note on this book 'Happiness with Success', I consider, is a special personal privilege and blessing.

Success without happiness is short-lived and incomplete. The Pandavas won the battle of Kurukshetra. But that victory did not bring them happiness. Alexander the Great won the victory. But he died in sorrow when he realized that his victory was meaningless. Many of the giants of the business world have faced failure in their personal lives. Some of the most talented artists wandered in search of happiness and at the end committed suicide.

Some of those who have reached the podium in the world of sports have later lost their happiness. There are also some rare personalities who have reached the ideal level of being happy even if they are not successful. Their number will be limited.

When India gained independence, Gandhi was initially happy with the successful conclusion of his non-violent struggle. But that happiness did not last long when India was partitioned. Political leaders celebrate victory when their party comes to power; But that success is only superficial if it is not possible to provide good governance for the people; that happiness is fleeting; and imperfect.

During my MBA studies at Cochin University's (now CUSAT) School of Management, I was an introvert. Professor Poduval helped me to realize my strengths and weaknesses as a person by a psychometric test developed by him. The training at the School of management proved to be a turning point in my professional career, and later when I started my own firm. It was that training that enabled me to give constructive leadership to a forty employee based strong organization, for 25 years.

The process of personality development has been explained in a simple way in the book *'Manassum Vyakthithwa vikasanavum'* ('Mind and Personality Development') written by Prof. Poduval. Let me quote it here:

Love yourself

> *Love others*

> *Loving others*

will flow by itself towards you.

> *If you have self-respect*

> *Others will respect you.*

> *Good relationship with others*

Will generate self confidence.

> *Have faith in your own behaviour*

> *For your confident living*

The formula for creating warm personal relationships can be read in these lines.

In the new book 'Happiness with Success' the author has described and explained complex psychology in a simple way. The chapters are arranged in ascending order which gives a different reading experience. This book will be of immense benefit and inspiration to psychology students, teachers, managers, social workers, political leaders, followers and everyone who is leading a family life.

Real success is achievement of goals (effectiveness) with efficiency without sacrificing social and ethical values. Such a success brings happiness. Then success and happiness evolve into a dual phenomenon.

Wealth and status are not the criteria for success; rather, this text affirms that they should be the consequences of success. The book leads the reader step by step forward through psychological principles, personality development theories and psychometric techniques, providing a unique reading experience.

In this modern age we live, we are overwhelmed by the unprecedented growth of technology.

It is to be suspected that personal and social relationships are shrinking as communication techniques become more complex. It can be seen that mobile phones, internet and social media create a situation where individuals are drawn into self confinement. Each of us should be prepared for a self-analysis to survive this situation. A comprehensive study of personality, interpersonal relationships and psychometric evaluation can be helpful in finding answers and solutions to this problem. I hope, this book 'Happiness with Success' will be a guide for it.

Recently, there was a press report on the findings of a research student of the Chemistry department of the Cochin University of science and Technology. The finding was that the level of the hormone 'dopamine' in the human body can be considered as an index of a person's happiness. Clinically, looking at hormone levels can be helpful in diagnosis. However, this method does not seem to be useful for understanding a person's mood, behaviour and attitudes. Only through some psychometric tests, one can know the stability of a person's mind, preferences and personality itself. The theories of personality presented in this book 'Happiness with successes' asserts that clinical observations without reliable and valid tests are not useful for the diagnosis of psychopathological conditions.

When we think of people who have achieved happiness with success, certain thoughts come to mind. One of the characteristics of their personality is that they motivate others through radiation of their energy. It was the combination of success and happiness that make them energised for this kind of motivation.

Known as Metroman, Sree. E. Sridharan, a talented engineer, achieved a rare feat when he rebuilt the Pampan Bridge. He turned the difficult Konkan Railway project into a historic success. The success story continued with completion of Delhi Metro and metro rail projects in other cities, saving time and money. He felt self-satisfaction and happiness in all these successes. Happiness and success were like a two-petalled flower for him.

Justice K. Sukumaran is the Bhishmacharya of the judicial world. Retired after distinguished service in the High Courts of Kerala and Maharashtra, he has been very active in literary and socio-cultural fields. I have felt the energy flowing into me whenever I interacted with Justice Sukumaran. He is a distinguished personality who has achieved happiness along with success.

A basic knowledge of human psychology, particularly on why people behave the way they do, would eliminate conflicts and behavioural antagonism and may also help to build proactive relationships. Administering personality test on candidates at the time of recruitment could be immensely useful in selecting the right candidate for the right job and also improving the selected candidates in their career path. We have been using Prof. Poduval's personality test for recruiting technologists to our laboratory for the last 15 years which we found beneficial for the organization as well as for the candidates.

A Short Review of the Book

Dr. C.J. Joseph

Former Principal,

Udyogamandal School

&

Life Member, Association of Schools of Indian School Certificate

(ASISC) - New Delhi

"Happiness with Success" is an excellent book by Prof. P.R. Poduval. It contains useful lessons for everyone.

With plenty of references and a rich glossary, the book is a thesis that will be of great benefit to students of psychology, management and other fields of study.

The psychometric tests he has referred to and especially the one he has brought out Poduval's Personal Efficacy Test (PPET) will be of immense benefit for self assessment as well as for selection procedures to various management positions. I sincerely congratulate him for his great achievement in bringing out this book.

Preface

The title of this book is 'Happiness with Success, and not, 'Happiness and Success'. Another possible title to this book could be 'The psychology of 'SREYAS'. The Sanskrit word *sreyas* carry the meaning that happiness with success is not a transient phenomenon; it is a sustained mental condition of attaining the desired goal with a feeling of satisfaction and well-being. Attaining a desired goal without any consideration for the social norms, ethics and efficiency will be only a temporary phenomenon -- some material prosperity without a feeling of satisfaction and a sense of wellness. And such a phenomenon in Sanskrit is termed as 'PREYAS', an attainment of the desired goal without a feeling of sustained happiness, which in turn will make the success a temporary one. *Sreyas* is greatness with goodness and wellness where as *Preyas* is greatness without goodness and wellness. The psychological factors associated with *Sreyas* or 'happiness with success' are discussed in detail in this book.

The proposition, 'All Happy persons are successful persons' logically implies (an immediate inference) that 'some successful persons are happy persons' and certainly not 'All successful persons are happy persons'. There cannot be a single proposition 'All happy persons are (all) successful persons'; it could be two propositions with a conjunction 'and' -- 'All happy persons are successful persons and all successful persons are happy persons'. There cannot be a syllogistic mediate inference from these two propositions as there is no common middle term connecting 'success' and 'happiness'. The two propositions with the conjunction may imply that 'success' and 'happiness' are one and the same phenomenon as both completely overlap without any differentiation. It is similar to 'x' is equal to 'y' and 'y' is equal to 'x' and because of this undifferentiating nature, such a statement as "All Happy persons are (all) successful persons", is never considered as a logical proposition.

The four valid logical propositions are: (1) Universal affirmative or 'A' proposition, such as 'All happy persons are successful persons', with its logical converse, 'Some successful persons are happy persons'. (2) Universal negative proposition or 'E' proposition, such as 'No Happy persons are successful persons'. The converse of this statement is 'No successful persons are happy persons' implying that each of them is independent without any connection. (3) Particular affirmative proposition or 'I' proposition: 'Some happy persons are successful persons' and its converse is, 'Some successful persons are happy persons'. It is the intersecting area of two circles labelled 'Happiness' and 'Success'; 'Happiness with success' or 'Success with Happiness' is this intersecting area. The non intersecting areas are two unconnected areas of 'success' and 'happiness'. The 4th logical proposition is Particular negative proposition or 'O' proposition, such as 'some happy persons are not successful persons'. One cannot directly converse this proposition by changing the position of subject and predicate as it will commit the fallacy of illicit minor or fallacy of illicit major i.e. from 'some' to 'all' is not valid, though from 'all' to 'some' is valid.

The only acceptable proposition for identifying the link between Happiness and success is the particular affirmative 'I' proposition wherein there are three categories of people viz; (1) some happy persons are successful persons and some successful persons are happy persons, (2) Some successful persons are not happy persons and (3) some happy persons are not successful persons. The first category of people is the *sreyas* group; the second category of people is the *Preyas* group and the third category is a happy *self actualizing* people without expecting any material prosperity for themselves by their actions.

If we want to exclude the third category of people i.e. the self sacrificing group for self actualization, we may have to redefine the meaning of 'success' from material prosperity of 'possessions' and 'positions' by achievement of the set goal by the individual concerned rather than the goals set by others for the individuals in the society.

The definitions of the concepts of 'happiness' and 'success' are discussed in detail under chapter 1 of this book.

The two concepts *'Sreyas'* and *'Preyas'* are taken from the 'Kathopanishad'. *'Sreyas'*, as per 'Kathopanishad', is the consequence of a lasting nature whereas *'preyas'* refers to the consequence that provide immediate pleasure to the self without any long term benefits of goodness and wellness.

The differentiation of *'sreyas'* and *'preyas'* becomes clear by taking the case of 'Kaikeyi' in Ramayana mythology. 'Kaikeyi', the third young wife of Raja Dasaratha, was a good character showing true motherly affection towards Rama. But, at one stage in her life, she changed her orientation from *'sreyas'* to *'preyas'* for getting positions and possessions by the desire to make her son the future Raja of 'Ayodhya' so that she would enjoy the status of the mother queen of the State. This shift of orientation from *'sreyas'* to *'preyas'* had its own negative impact on her outlook and attitude – instead of being happy, she became unhappy throughout her life on the banishment of Rama from Ayodhya.

All behaviour (behaviour includes writing, speaking, actions etc.), has a background. Why did I write this book? I have the background of studying psychology and becoming a psychology teacher at the university level and then a teacher in Human Relations in a Management School of another university. This book is the culmination of my research and teaching background for developing excellent managers and also an additional responsibility of selecting and training managers of excellent competence and confidence.

There are many individuals and institutions that have inspired me to write this book. The first name that comes to my mind is my close friend Shri. P. Padmanabhan, who knew my educational background and professional achievements. He constantly persuaded me to write this book. He read the chapter-wise manuscript and pointed out the areas that needed to be changed for better clarity.

He worked as a scientist in the Quality Assurance Establishment under the department of Defence Production. Now he is living a retired life in Pune.

Former Director of Naval Physical and Oceanographic Laboratory (NPOL, Kochi), Engineer-scientist Sri. S. Ananthanarayan was very kind to me in going through the manuscript so as to make it more appealing to the readers. When I requested him to write the foreword to this book, he readily agreed. Sri. Ananthanarayan is a friend, philosopher and guide to several science oriented youths through his publications on science topics in Malayalam. His 'thapasya' after his retirement from service is academic services to the science oriented youth. Let me express my gratitude and thanks to him.

Dr. K. Babu Joseph, former vice-Chancellor of Cochin University of Science and Technology (CUSAT), and a well-known writer in Malayalam on Physics and related academic disciplines, was very kind in writing his comments on my work. I take this opportunity to express my respectful thanks to Dr. Babu Joseph.

Dr. B.J. Meledom, CEO and founder director of M/s Synergy Systems, Kochi, has expressed his appreciation of the book. Dr. Meledom is a voracious reader of both Malayalam and English books and it is his love for creative writings that prompted him to write the appreciation.

Dr. C.J. Joseph, deserves special thanks for polishing my words and expressions in English, in addition to his short review of the book.

All those who worked for the end product of this book – the artist who designed the cover page, an expert on computer Shree RBS Madhavan who helped me with his services in preparing the manuscript, the press personnel of Notion Press, Chennai, the publisher, my son Mr. Subhash chandran and other family members and all others who supported me in my efforts –- are gratefully acknowledged with thanks and appreciation.

Prof. P. Ramachandra Poduval

'Thapasya', No. 11, Vidyanagar, Kochi-682022

Chapter 1

Happiness with Success

Happiness means ....

Pleasant and unpleasant events are part of our life. That which is pleasing to the senses and the mind is pleasant and painful things are unpleasant. Shall we describe all unpleasant things as sorrow? When the intensity of an unpleasant experience is high, then we may say it as sorrowful or an emotional sadness.

Pleasantness also has many facets. These words (satisfaction, happiness, joy and bliss) have reference to these levels of emotion. Feeling of pleasure when eating a favourite food is satisfaction; the height of that satisfaction is satiation; Happiness is the pleasant feeling when all the expected outcomes are attained. A high intensity of pleasantness for a short duration is joy; a sustained well-being can be called happiness with the thought that life's purpose is meaningful. According to the Positive psychologists, wellness or feeling of well-being is the essence of happiness (Crompton, W.C. and Hoffmann, E. 2012; Diener, Ed. And Diener, R.B. 1996; Agarwal, J. 1985; Warr, Peter. 2019).

Although there are a great deal of research on the emotions of individuals, differences in their levels of expression raise many questions -- especially the differences between satisfaction, and happiness. In the words of Martin Seligman, a positive psychologist, there are three types of happiness in life (1) a pleasant life (2) a good life, and (3) a meaningful life. True happiness lies in this third category of happiness. A meaningful life is the foundation for success with happiness (Saligman M.E.P., 2002)

Success means........

If a desired goal is achieved, then, it can be called success. Many people assume that a person's possessions and positions are signs of his/her success. It may not be correct to say that the criterion of success is possessions and positions. Possessions and positions are the consequences of success, not the causes. Achievement of the desired goal is the only measure of success (Ref: Deborah, A. O. 2017).

If achievement of the desired goal is the sole criterion, then it is only a temporary success. Two additional criteria are necessary if success is to be sustained. (1) Efficiency (2) Respect for social values of non-exploitation of others. The term 'efficiency' refers not only to performance skills, but also to punctuality, doing more in less time, and not using more resources than required. Efficiency is not only a process but also a product. Don't call people as winners by the result achieved alone, without looking at efficiency and social values. Those who get things done somehow by any means without any consideration for social values and efficiency are successful only for a short period, not sustainable (Ref: Deborah, A.O., 2017.) Happiness is for those who achieve sustainable success (Dweck., C.S., 2006). Success without happiness is '*Preyas*' and it is not '*Sreyas*'. Happiness with success is '*Sreyas*'. '*Preyas*' is not sustained in the long run; '*Sreyas*' is both a sustained success and a sustained happiness (Ref: Misra, S., 2018).

True Happiness with success, is the achievement of desired goal by adherence to three criteria: effectiveness, efficiency and commitment to social values. (Baron, J. 2000.; Covey. S.R. 1989.)

Relationship between happiness and success:

The title of this book is Happiness with success. Can there be success without happiness? Is happiness possible without success?

Is success a consequence of happiness or happiness a consequence of success? Or, do they both happen together? These are questions that deserve detailed study. A true answer to this issue lies in the definitions of 'success' and 'happiness'. The definitions of these words have been given at the beginning of the book. Success is goal achievement; not just an achievement, but an achievement with efficiency and an achievement without exploiting others. If this is the definition of 'success', then happiness and success are concepts that always go together. To a common man, a successful person is one with name, status and resources. Such successful persons may or may not be happy, depending on other conditions. But, when we redefine the concept 'success' as a condition of achievement of goals or effectiveness with efficiency and without sacrificing social values, then happiness is bound to follow success. Effectiveness means attainment of the goal. The goal can be name, status, or resource mobilization, or it could be anything. Success is based on one common thing-- goal attainment or effectiveness. Name, fame, wealth, etc. are not the criteria of success, but the consequences of success.

Just listen to the statements on success and happiness pronounced by well known personalities:

> Action may not always bring happiness, but there is no
> happiness without action.

– (James, W. 1902)

The following statements are attributed as pronouncement of Shri. Buddha (quotable quotes from internet):

"There is no path to happiness. Happiness is the path."

"One who acts on truth is happy in this world and beyond."

"If with a pure mind a person speaks or acts, happiness follows him like his never-departing shadow."

"Happiness will never come to those who fail to appreciate what they already have."

"A disciplined mind brings happiness."

"If your desire is to soar high, drop everything that weighs you down".

"If you want others to be happy, practice compassion. If you want to be happy, practice compassion".

– Dalai Lama (1999)

"Happiness is when what you think, what you say, and what you do are in harmony."

– *(Gandhi, M.K., 1927)*

"Happiness is not something ready- made; It comes from your own actions"

– (Maslow, A.H., 1954)

"Success is not the key to happiness; happiness is the key to success".

– (Schweitzer, A., 1992)

I am not a product of my circumstances. I am a product of my decisions.

– (Covey, S.R., 1989)

Happiness Index:

Today many countries are trying to implement reforms to increase the number of individuals who experience success with happiness from 20 percent to 80 percent. For this, the first step is to find a measurement of happiness. Today, the socio-economic prosperity of the people of a country is measured through the Human Resource Development Index (HDI,). HDI shows which country is better in health, education and economic status. (Ref: UNDP Report on Human Development index, 2022.) Bhutan, a country in the Himalayas, has taken initiative in developing the concept of Gross National Happiness (GNH). Following this concept of GNH, the Happiness Index was developed by the

United Nations. Social support, income, health, freedom, generosity, and absence of corruption are the main factors associated with the Happiness Index. (Ref: UN Sustainable Development: World happiness Index, 2023).

Per capita income is a common factor found in the Human Development Index, the National Happiness Index, and the economic level per capita (PPP in US dollars for comparison). So it is possible to see more similarities in rank positions among these three categories – per capita income, Human Development Index and Human Happiness Index. There are many countries that show backwardness in all three --- Burundi, Afghanistan, Sierra Leone, Malawi, South Sudan, Yemen etc. The U.S.A, Qatar, Singapore, Australia, and Ireland which are at the top in the per capita income level, do not find a place at the top ten countries in the Happiness Index -- although Ireland and Australia are there in the top ten in the Human Development Index (UN reports, 2022., 2023., Forbes India, 2023)

In other words, not all countries with the best economic status, are at top in the happiness index. Norway, Sweden, Finland, Denmark and Switzerland are all ahead of USA, Qatar, Singapore, etc. (Ref: UN sustainable Development Solutions Network Report, 2023; UNDP Report on HDI, 2022; Forbesindia.com, 2023) Those nations, who curb excessive desires and achieve a mind set to lead a meaningful life, are at the top in the rank list of the happiness index.

Mind is a phenomenon; but, life is a paradox:

What is the difference between a phenomenon and a paradox/ conundrum? Both can be described. But, a paradox/conundrum is beyond analysis and explanation. Conundrum is a riddle --- something that cannot be explained--- or a paradox – something with contradictory explanations. A phenomenon is something that can be scientifically understood through analysis and explanation. Events that once seemed to be a conundrum/paradox/enigma may become phenomena. Many mental phenomena that cannot be seen or heard have been scientifically studied and understood through practical operational definitions. Yesterday's conundrum is today's phenomenon; Today's phenomenon is tomorrow's scientific fact.

Many people think that success in life is an enigma or conundrum. Have you not heard someone say that they have talent but no luck? Others say that time is not good even if they are lucky and talented. If something cannot be understood by a scientific analysis, it is not a phenomenon, but a conundrum/paradox. This book is an attempt at understanding the phenomenon of happiness with success through a scientific way---through modern psychology.

The chemistry of behaviour dispositions:

Many things can happen in life at the same time. Instead of holding to the principle that a thing has only one clear cause, consider that a thing can have multiple, mixed, or combined causes. In human nature, not only variations in one quality but the combination of two or more qualities can also result in a new behaviour pattern. High personal autonomy coupled with a feeling of high level of intimacy, results in assertive style in interpersonal relationship, whereas high personal autonomy with low level of intimacy results in dominative style of interpersonal behaviour. Such variations by permutations and combinations are possible in behaviour dispositions. The uniqueness of a person is the result of such combinations of traits and there is no special trait called uniqueness

Pareto's Law of 20/80:

Pareto's Law states that 20 out of 100 people produce 80% of the results. Out of the remaining 100, 80 people give 20 percent results only (Koch, R and Lockwood G, 2013). That is, all the good and great things in the society are done by a minority of people. The essence is that the world is always ruled by the minority. What would the world be like if this benevolent minority became the majority? Not only that the rate of failure will decrease but the number of under-skilled people will also drop sharply. When the number of competent individuals increases from 20 percent to 80 percent, the number of incompetents decreases from 80 to 20 percent. In other words, the success rate will jump from 20 percent to a significant higher level. The effort of all socio-economic and other reforms is to attain this kind of transformation.

What you may expect in this book:

Although life is a paradox, Happiness with success should be considered as a phenomenon for description and explanation. The theme of this book is the psychological analysis and explanation of this phenomenon. Let's try to change the fact of 20 percent people producing 80 percent results into 80 percent people producing a high level of desired results. Only a small percentage of people are to be incompetent and ineffective in a desirable society. This book also describes the practical aspect of transforming the ineffective 80 percent into an effective 80%. Major propositions on happiness with success and the essential contents of each chapter of this book are given below:

1. Phenomenon Y is the function of X is the basic assumption for the identification of the causation factor. In addition, when other factors combined with X factor, it t in either as a mixture or as a compound and the new product may become a new behaviour pattern or a style.

2. wealth and status (possessions and positions) are not criteria for success in life; they are only the consequences of success in life.

3. Sustained success in life can only be achieved if three criteia are adopted, i.e. achievement of purpose or effectiveness, efficiency, and code of conduct based on social values. The term 'Sreyas' refers to this sustained success in life. The word 'Prayas' refers to temporary success and gain that are not sustainable in the long run.

4. There are some mindsets that hinder happiness with success; similarly, there are mindsets that facilitate happiness with success. This book goes into detail about such mindsets that foster or hinder the phenomenon of happiness with success of

human beings. Psychologically acceptable methods to overcome or modify the mindset that hinders happiness with success are discussed in detail in subsequent chapters.

5. The first chapter of the book is an introduction to 'Happiness and Success'

6. The second chapter describes psychological principles and theories of personality and personal development.

7. Chapter 3 focuses on the contributions of modern positive psychology, particularly on happiness and success.

8. What are the psychological qualities or traits associated with happiness with success? How they are measured and what are the theoretical and practical aspects of such measurements? Such issues are discussed in detail in the fourth chapter.

9. The 566-item Minnesota Multiphasic Personality Inventory (MMPI) was subjected to empirical research for their relevance to the Indian (kerala) normal human adults. By such efforts, the items were reduced to 92 (college-educated men and women over 19 years of age). Several subscales relevant to the selection of managerial personnel were taken for standardization in the Indian context. All details relating to this work and the final products of 10 subscales are discussed in detail in the fifth chapter.

10. The psychology of interpersonal relationships is covered in Chapter 6;

11. social relationships and leadership qualities are discussed in Chapter 7;

12. The theme of the 8th chapter is the 'Transactional Analysis' and 'Life Positions';

13. Communication with empathy is at the focus of the 9th chapter

14. Emotional state in the process of decision making and implementation is at the focus of the 10th chapter.

15. The subject of the 11th chapter is 'Personal Efficacy'. The concept of personal efficacy is very similar to the concept of self efficacy of Albert Bandura, but different in terms of its scope and applications. The essence of managerial competence is this concept of personal efficacy--- a combined effect of two factors of personality i.e. People orientation and Performance orientation

16. Other aspects of the mindset other than personal efficacy associated with 'Happiness with Success' are discussed in the final chapter titled as 'Epilogue'.

Attention to details, verbal fluency, urban sophistication, time management etc are the extra aspects other than personal efficacy. Authentic and objective personal interview method will be sufficient to assess such secondary mindsets.

Ways and means to overcome the behaviour characteristics for better wellbeing by training and counselling are also discussed in this final chapter.

Glossary of Terms:

Conundrum: An object/event/ situation which can be described, but cannot be explained on a scientific cause – effect relations; a riddle or puzzle that is beyond rational explanation.

Effectiveness: a state or condition of goal achievement.

Efficacy: power or competence to be effective and efficient without sacrificing social and ethical values.

Efficiency: economy in time, effort and utilization of resources.

Happiness: a sustained state or condition of wellness or a mental feeling of well being.

Happiness Index (HI): An index designed by the United Nations to assess the level of well being experienced by the people of a nation.

Happiness with success: Sreyas or a sustained prosperity with high level of well being as the state of the mind.

Human Development Index (HDI): An index designed by the United Nations to assess the level of human development by taking into account, (1) per capita income (economic status) (2) years of schooling (education) and (3) life expectancy (health)

Mindset: The mental framework of a person with predisposed ideas/ beliefs/ action tendencies.

Paradox: Something that cannot be explained by scientific reasoning; objects, events or situations. There could be contradictory explanations to such events

Pareto's law: 80 percent of the result obtained is caused by 20 percent of people or it is always the minority who contribute the maximum results.

Personal efficacy: competent and confident behaviour disposition of a person.

Personality traits: Behaviour dispositions or tendency to act in a particular manner by the push of the past experiences.

Phenomenon: The singular form of the plural 'phenomena' i.e. object/situation/event under observation which is to be explained by scientific reasoning and empirical experiments.

Preyas: Life success/Material prosperity without a feeling of happiness; the focus is on pleasure for a short duration, not a sustained positive feelings.

Psychometric tests: Quantitative, objective measurement of behaviour dispositions or personality traits by use of standardized tests.

Social values: The concept of the right things to do or behave approved and accepted by the community or society. Deviations from such social values and norms are disapproved by social isolation/rejection.

Sreyas: Sustained material prosperity with happiness for a longer duration; greatness with goodness and wellness in human behaviour.

Success: For ordinary people, success is earning of name and fame by achieving material possessions and positions; the use of this term in this book is confined to effectiveness (achievement of the desired goal) with efficiency without exploiting others. Such a success will be a sustained success and not a transient one for an immediate purpose.

Success with Happiness: The overlapping area of happiness and success circles – The sreyas area with sustained happiness along with success.

References:

Agrawal, Jyothsna (1985).,

Aananda and Sukha: Indian Model of Happiness.

New Delhi: Vikas Publishing House.

Baron, J. (2000).,

Thinking and Deciding, (3rd Ed.).

New York: Cambridge University Press.

Covey, S.R. (1989).,

The 7 Habits of Highly Effective People.

California: Free Press.

Compton, William C. And Hoffmann, E. (2012).,

Positive Psychology: The Science of happiness and Flourishing.

California: Wadsworth Publishing.

Dalai Lama (1999).,

The Art of Happiness at Work.

U.K.: Hodder Paperbacks

Deborah, A.O. (Ed.) 2017.,

Success: The Psychology of Achievement.,

U.K.: DK Publishers.

Diener, Ed and Diener R.B. (2008).,

Happiness: Unlocking the Mysteries of Psychological Wealth.

NJ: Wiley --online Library.

Dweck, C.S. (2006).,

Mindset: The New Psychology of Success.

New York: Random House.

Forbesindia.com (Internet).,

Top Ten Richest Countries in the world, 2023.

Mumbai, India.

Gandhi, M.K. (1927).,

An autobiography: The Story of My Experiments with Truth.

Ahmedabad, India: Navajeevan Publishing House.

James, William. (1902).,

The Varieties of Religious Experience.

Cambridge: Harvard University Press.

Koch, R and Lockwood, G (2013).,

The 80/20 Manager: Ten Ways to become a Great Leader.

U.K.: Little Brown.

Maslow, A.H. (1957).,

Motivation and Personality.

NY: Harper & Row.

Misra, S. (2018).,

Two Paths: Sreyas and Preyas

Bhagavath Gita (Blog), 25 March, 2018.

http://bhagavathgita.org.in /Blogs/ ....

Seligman, Martin, E.P. (2002).,

Authentic Happiness,

New York: Free Press.

Schweitzer, A. (1992).,

The Philosophy of civilization.

NY: Prometheus Books.

UNDP

Human Development Report, 2022.

UN Sustainable Development Solutions Network

World Happiness Index, 2023.

Warr, Peter (2019).,

The Psychology of Happiness.

U.K.: Rutledge.

Chapter 2

The Person and his/her Personality

The Concept of Personality:

A person is a Psycho-social being. Should a comprehensive study of a person be called Personality or Personology? According to the famous psychologist Henry Murray, the word 'personology' is preferable. (Murray, H.A. and Christiana Morgan, 1938). The term 'Personality' has a connotation of social desirability and such an evaluative judgment should not be a part of the definition of a concept for a detailed scientific study. Therefore, the term 'Personology' is more appropriate. But, as the use of the word 'personality' was better established, Murray's new use of the word did not receive enough attention and appreciation. The opinion that there is no difference between the person and the personality and that both are one and the same is not only the opinion of Henry Murray, but also of the psychologist Sigmund Freud and his followers of different shades of psychoanalysis (Adler Alfred; Jung, C.G.; Karen Horney; Erich Fromm; Erik Erikson). In order to understand a person's behaviour and personality, it is necessary to open the storehouse of the person's unconscious motivations and emotions or the psychodynamics as Freud called such forces. According to G.W. Allport, the behavioural characteristics of a person that create a uniqueness in the person is the personality of that person (Allport, G.W. 1937;1961). Allport's opinion seems to be good; but there is no clarity about what this speciality called uniqueness is. When many qualities are put together, certain compound products may emerge. Apart from that, there is no other special characteristic or temperament. There are many physical and mental personality traits or behaviour dispositions. Combinations of such traits may result in certain behavioural styles. Let's now explore various theories that explain the behavioural characteristics or personality pattern/profile of individuals.

1. Sigmund Freud (1856–1939):

According to the theory of Sigmund Freud, the founder of psychoanalytic school of thought, a person has three levels of personality structure: Id, the innate wishful thinking of a being; the sense of reality or ego that comes from social interactions; Moral thoughts or superego derived from the advices given by parents, family members, neighbouring elders and teachers (Freud, S. 2011).

Our behaviour is based on these three inner psychological structures. Occasionally, there can be conflicts between these three structural levels-- Between Id and Ego; between the ego and the superego, between the id and the superego. In such conflicts, if one is a winner, the other must be a loser. The loser will either go away by suppression or hide inside by repression for doing many unwanted things. The repressed wishes are known as emotionally charged mental 'complexes'. We will be conscious of it if the loser leaves the scene by suppression; if the loser hides inside, then, we may not be aware of its presence as it functions at the unconscious level, though we are aware of its behavioural consequences. It is always the ego that makes everything conscious or aware of. The id and the superego are always function at the unconscious level. The 'Unconscious' is the result of repression to resolve the conflict. Dreams, psychopathology in everyday life such as forgetting the names of familiar persons or things for a short period, and mental disorders are the result of such psycho-dynamics and defence mechanisms (Freud, S., 2019., 2021)

Freud pointed out the difference between what is consciously covered up (suppression) and what is repressed from the conscious level and acts at the unconscious level (repression). Suppression may result in an unpleasant experience at first, but will be neutral later. In the case of repressed wishes, one may experience temporary relief, but later it will lead to some pathological behaviour.

Freud calls the temporary relief from repression as ego defence mechanisms. Attributing one's faults and shortcomings to others (projection), justifying one's own behaviour at all costs (rationalization) etc., are self-protection strategies. Freud says nothing about behavioural traits or personality. Psychoanalytic theory provides certain explanations for the exhibited behaviour.

In the Freudian theory, the energy of the mind of individuals flows in two ways: The 'Life instinct' (constructive and creative way) or The 'Death instinct' (destructive way). A man can be a god or a demon; can be healthy or sick. Everything depends on the activity of the mind. It is the unconscious functioning of the mind that is assumed to be the cause of much unexplainable behaviour. Libido is the main source of mental energy. For Freud, 'Libido' is basically sex energy. It is life energy for other mental philosophers. To Freud, Libido, the sex energy, is nothing but body pleasure evoked at different parts of the body at different stages in life. This concept of psychosexual development from oral stage to heterosexual stage is the reference in this context. (Freud, S., 1962). It is this very concept of sex energy that is the main cause of criticism as well as praise for the Freudian theory. One thing needs to be clarified here: all body desires are sexual in Freudian view. At each stage of development, the sex drive resides at different levels and this is well explained in Freudian theory of psychosexual development (Freud. S., 1962). This is also where Freud's mental structure, the 'id', comes into play. It is the duty of the reality oriented 'Ego' to intervene for the control of sex energy with a sense of social awareness. Ego does not mean self or arrogance; it is a Freudian concept of a mental structure that controls the reality orientation of a person.

There are writers, painters, and other artists who talk about psychology as if psychology is Freudian psychoanalysis. This may be due to their limited knowledge of modern psychology.

Freud's theories are significant contributions to psychology; but there are differences in views on some conceptual aspects. One of them is the claim that childhood experiences are the main cause of all current mental problems. Other psychologists do not accept the argument that past experiences are more powerful than recent experiences, although the power of experience is an important factor. Even Freud's closest colleagues were not ready to accept all his arguments. This becomes clear when we examine the theories of Alfred Adler, Carl Gustav Jung, Karen Horney, Erik Erikson, and Erich Fromm. The idea that the person is the personality is reinforced by the theories put forward by these famous neo Freudians.

2. Alfred Adler (1870–1937):

In Alfred Adler's school of thought, libido is not sex energy; it is just a passion for life or life energy. Our behavior is mostly controlled by the social environment, especially the psychological environment within the family. (Adler, A., 1927 social/family emphasis) The character of the child depends on how the family members (father, mother, brothers and sisters, grandparents etc) treat the child. A child who is very helpless in comparison with others must acquire certain skills to free himself/herself from the thought of helplessness. It is in this context that Adler used technical terms such as 'inferiority complex' and 'masculine protest' (Adler, A. 1964).) The person struggles to show that he/she is strong in order to overcome the feelings of inferiority—similar to a student who performs poorly in studies excels in sports. It is at this early age that the self/ego concept of "me" is born.

Children's behavior is based on the discrimination shown by parents and others in the family. The first born child may exhibit an authoritarian/dominating behavior; the last born child may be meek, dependent or a submissive one loved by all; Children born in the middle are likely to be rebels or outspoken revolutionaries. Character formation of these types is a special contribution of the family drama. Later, Karen Horney and Erich Fromm reinforced these ideas of Alfred Adler.

3. Carl Gustav Jung (1875–1961):

C.G. Jung, a Swiss psychiatrist, was a close associate of Sigmund Freud in the early stage of the development of the Freudian school of psychoanalysis. But, difference of views on many ideas of Freud led Jung to form his own distinct school known as the Analytic psychology. For Freud, libido is sex energy or pleasures derived from various parts of the body whereas Jung assumes that libido is the life energy that gets reflected in all activities of human beings. Jung assumed another unconscious region of human personality i.e. 'collective unconscious', in addition to the concept of Freudian 'personal unconscious' structure of the mind (Jung, C.G., (1925). The contents of the collective unconscious are parts of the mental structure and they are termed as 'archetypes' by Jung. The feminine part of man is termed as the anima and the masculine part of women is termed as animus. The half man- half women concept within a single person as conceived in Siva personality is akin to the archetype of anima and animus of Jungian analytic school. 'Persona' or the mask of well accepted and approved social man is another archetype; 'Shadow' is the dark side of personality hidden from others. The 'self' is another concept within the broad band of archetypes. Archetypes are essentially symbolic expressions of certain common ideas evolved in the history of mankind (Jung, C.G., 1959., 1964) 'Personal unconscious' is developed from an individual life history and the 'collective unconscious' is developed from the history of mankind; both are influencing the behavior of individuals without being conscious to the person. Many ideas of Jung are highly influential in religion and with a lot of similarities with the Indian Philosophy.

Another important concept of Jung is the flow of libido or life energy either inside the individual or outside. When the life energy flows within the individual, it is called 'Introversion' and the flow if towards external matters, it is 'extroversion' (Jung, C.G., 1933). Each of these two energy flows are further subdivided into 'Thinking', 'Feeling', 'Intuitive' and 'Judgmental' types. The well-known M.B.T.I. (Myers-Briggs Type Indicator) psychological test was built on the eight personality types put forward by C.G. Jung.

4. Eric Erikson (1902–1994):

Sigmund Freud elaborated the concept of psychosexual development in terms of oral, anal, phallic, no sex interest, homosexual and heterosexual stages. Eric Erikson focused attention on psycho-social development stages and their impact on personality. He assumed that there are eight critical stages in which two opposing forces are trying to win over by a conflict resolutions:

1. Early infancy stage from birth to 18 months. During this stage, the child gets warmth and love from the mother. It is this love and warmth from the mother that creates a sense of trust and absence of this love and warmth from the mother will result in mistrust. A conflict within the child between trust and mistrust is experienced during the early infancy stage depending on the attitude of the mother towards the child. If trust wins the conflict, the child when grows into an adult becomes optimistic and cordial in his relationship with others and if mistrust is the winner, then the person becomes a suspicious type who does not exhibit any trust in others. Intimacy with others in life has its origin in the mother child relations at the infancy stage.

2. The second stage of development from 2 years to 3 years: During this period the conflict is between 'Autonomy' and 'Doubt'. The child tries to do many things at its own initiative and success in such efforts results in psychological autonomy and failures in such attempts results in doubt in one's own competence.

3. The third stage from 3 years to 5 years: This is a continuation of the second stage in a different form and the conflict is between 'initiative' and 'guilt'/'shame'. Success in initiative in several activities, if supported by parents and others will result in confidence and failure will results in a feeling of 'guilt'/'shame'.

4. The fourth stage from 6 years to 11 years: This is the period of primary education. The child tries to excel in studies and it becomes a success or failure. The conflict is between 'Industry' and 'Inferiority'; success in industry will result in a feeling of higher self-esteem whereas failure will be the basis of inferiority.

5. The fifth stage from 12 years to 18 years/adolescence: Erickson's famous expression 'identity crisis' comes at this stage of development. An answer to the question 'who am I' is at this stage. If the person develops an identity of his/her own and feels

significant, he will be a happy person by his/her own standards. Failure to achieve this self-identity will result in a feeling of insignificance of self in all social and other life situations.

6. The sixth stage from 19 years to 49 years: This is a stage for developing intimacy with others or absence of the same. Professional advancement or lack of it is also during this period.

7. The period from 41 years to 65 years: here at this stage, the conflict is between 'generativity' and 'stagnation'. If generativity is the winner, then creative outputs in life is the consequence, otherwise it is stagnation or a depressive meaningless life.

8. The 8th and the final stage of psychosocial development from 65 years onwards: The conflict at this stage is between 'Integrity' and 'Despair'. Integrity implies happiness by a feeling that his/her life was a meaningful one; Despair is the opposite feeling of meaningless unwanted existence. The dawn of wisdom is also at this stage, if life was found meaningful. Eric Erickson assumes the healthy growth of personality is built on trust, autonomy, initiative, industry, self-identity, intimacy, generativity and integrity; unhealthy personality development is the result of mistrust, doubt, shame, inferiority, no sense of self identity, lack of intimacy, stagnation and despair (Eri Erikson, 1950.,1968., 1982)

5. Karen Horney (1885–1952):

Karen Horney's theory on interpersonal relationship is quite interesting. To Karen Hrney, birth is a great traumatic event; it is an unexpected transition from the comfortable womb of the mother to a new world of air ridden open world. This change will be a shocking experience to the child.

It is difficult to live in a hostile world consisting of self and others. Karen Horney calls the experienced insecurity of the child as 'Basic anxiety'. A person experiencing basic anxiety may adopt certain strategies to avoid the uncomfortable experience of anxiety. Three unhealthy ways of such strategies are: (1) Seeking refuge in others for protection (Moving Towards people) (2) Moving away from others for survival (Moving Away from people) (3) Attacking others before they attack (Moving Against people). These three strategies result in unhealthy interpersonal relationships. Positive healthy relationship can be established only by a fourth strategy of moving with others without much dependency on them. People who go to others to live in their shadow for security are generally submissive. Taking one's own decisions and actions is not within their will power.

The other two options are to blame others for your insecurities and either to avoid them or to act against them. Those who try the avoidance strategy will focus on becoming self-sufficient in all matters. Miserliness is also a part of such behaviour. People who work against others will be violent. They hurt others with their words or behaviour (Horney, K., 1950). Those who get along well with love and care for others are usually assertive with honest communication in interpersonal relationships.

At the social level, gaining the approval of others, loving and influencing others, and preserving self-sufficiency and autonomy for one's own survival and growth are the strategies to keep away the basic anxiety. Karen Horney's theory places more emphasis on interpersonal relationships and her advice is to understand the specifics of these relationships to analyse one's own behaviour, and to move toward people with love, care and considerations (Horney, K., 1942; 1945).

6. Erich Fromm (1900–1980):

Erich Fromm is better known as a social scientist who integrated the ideas of Karl Marx and Freud, rather than as a known Neo-Freudian. Fromm says that 'Humanistic Communistic Socialism' is the only solution to change many distortions and defects found in our society. Fromm explains the psychological principles behind such distortions and defects. According to Fromm, the five basic human needs are: (1) Relatedness to others (2) Rootedness with one's own past (3) Creativity to move from old to new (4) Identity as an independent person and (5) a productive structural mental framework known as Productive

Frame of Orientation. The mental health of a person will be perfect, if he/she can satisfy all these five basic human needs. Inability to satisfy these needs will result in many mental health problems (Fromm, Erich. 1941; 2005).

When thinking about frames of orientation, Fromm elaborates five types of frames. (1) Receptive orientation: Receptive orientation is an approach or behaviour disposition to make everything one's own; it is the desire for possessiveness (2) Exploitative orientation: an approach or disposition to make use of others for one's own benefits. (3) Hoarding orientation: the tendency to store for the future in order to avoid possible insecurities. It is another term for miserliness. (4) Marketing orientation: a tendency to look at everything for buying and selling for one's own benefits. It is a public relations personality. (5) Productive Orientation: an approach or disposition characterised by self-identity – independence from others and autonomy in taking decisions and actions without any desire for recognition and appreciation from others. Creative action is possible only by such freedom and identity (Fromm, Erich. 1976).

A totalitarian welfare State often makes people dependent subjugated followers, taking away their psychological freedom. This idea of psychological slavery was discussed in detail by Fromm in his book 'Escape from Freedom' (Fromm, Erich. 1941)

The humanistic approach in personal development was also underscored by Fromm. Abraham Maslow and Carl R. Rogers are the other known psychologists who stressed the importance of self actualization in the humanistic approach for the study of personality (Maslow, A. H., 1954., Rogers, C.R., 1951; 1961)

7. Allport G.W. (1897–1967):

G.W. Allport, a Harvard professor, is well known as the father of personality studies. Allport disagreed with Sigmund Freud's descriptive psychoanalytic approach, and he did not completely approve the views of Behaviorists Watson, Skinner and others who tried to explain behavior in term of the learning process alone. Allport was of the opinion that description of behavior alone is not sufficient; an explanation is required within a theoretical framework. He was of the opinion that it is not correct to interpret today's behavior by focusing on events that happened in the long past; We need to understand the dynamics of today's events associated with the exhibited behavior or behavior patterns. One of the right approaches is examining the behavior dispositions or personality traits functioning now as a consequence of past experiences. His focus was on this concepts of behavior pattern, behavior dispositions/personality traits, and the uniqueness of a person in terms of trait combinations known as personality profiles (Allport, G.W. 1961;1937). The traits may be physical, and mental (psycho-social, emotional etc.). He exlored the words of such traits in a dictionary and came to the conclusion that after excluding the synonyms, antonyms etc the total of such traits are reduced to 1800 words. Reducing a large number of qualities/traits into small essential ones based on the commonalities among such traits is known as 'Factor Analysis' in the science of statistics. Allport did not make use of the statistical technique of factor analysis, but other psychologists who came later in the field of personality made use of factor analysis to derive at latent factors among several correlated traits.

According to Allport, there are three types of traits. (1) Predominant or Cardinal Traits -- These traits are special unique characteristics of a person. (2) Central Traits--These are traits that are present in all individuals to a greater or lesser extent. (3) Secondary traits or minor traits found only in certain circumstances. Traits are not visible exhibited behavior; they are only disposition to behave in a predictable way or a 'mind set'.

Another concept that Allport emphasized is relevant here. That concept is 'Functional Autonomy'. Although an observed phenomenon (behavior) is initially associated with its cause, the behavior may later occur even in the absence of the initial cause. This is the speciality of habits. Such independent functions in the absence of its original cause can be found in many behavior dispositions or mind sets.

8. Cattell R.B., (1905–1998):

R.B. Cattell was a psychologist who narrowed down many traits to 16 source traits through factor analysis and established that these are the basic personality structure. External expressions of these traits are termed as surface traits and they are many in number. His 16 P.F. psychometric instrument is a powerful tool for the measurements of the basic personality structure. The 16 PF traits are listed in chapter 4 in the context of Psychometric tests available for use. Cattell, R.B, 1946; 1952)

9. Eysenck, H.J., (1916–1997):

H. J. Eysenck, a British psychologist put forward the two dimensional theory of personality: (1) Introversion--Extroversion. (2) Neuroticism (absence of emotional stability). Earlier, he had mentioned a third dimension of 'psychoticism' which he discarded later. Personality traits can be placed at a place on the combination of these two dimensions. There can be an extroverted emotional stability trait or an introverted emotional stability trait; an extroverted neuroticism or an introverted neuroticism. Cattell's stress was on traits whereas Eyesenck emphasised 'types' which is at a higher order to 'traits'. At the lowest level is a specific behaviour; a cluster of correlated behaviours becomes a 'trait' and a cluster of traits becomes a 'type' (Eysenck, H.J., 1959., 1947). Although some objections were raised later on the research work of Eysenck, his contributions based on factor analysis, are to be acknowledged.

10. Albert Bandura (1925–2021):

The theory put forward by the Canadian psychologist Albert Bandura is known as 'Social Cognitive Theory'. A person learns by observing and imitating the things that happen within his/her perceptual field. Learning by observation and imitation is called 'modelling', and it is through this process that the individual adjusts his/her own behaviour to the demands of his/her environment. Bandura's theory is very helpful for personality development. Bandura also talks about the phenomenon of self-efficacy. His self-efficacy theory states that a person is primarily responsible for his/ her success in life. Personal efficacy is a system of belief of the person that he/she is competent in accomplishment of tasks assigned or problems solved or decision taken (Bandura, A., 1997., 1977; 1969).

11. Albert Ellis (1913–2007):

Albert Ellis was a psychologist who developed a treatment system called REBT (Rational Emotive Behaviour Therapy). In his view, rational thinking can control emotional behaviour. Our emotions are based on our thoughts and perceptions. REBT is built on the inextricable relationship between rational thoughts and emotional feelings. An example is given below:

Close friends may use abuse language to each other when they are alone in an informal setting and such words are indication of their intimacy. But, use of such expressions in the presence of others will be misinterpreted as indication of hostility. Such interpretations are closely associated with emotions and feelings. Similarly, the feeling by seeing a snake that suddenly appears on the road is not the same as looking at a snake in a zoo. The essence of REBT is such differences in interpretations of a given situation. Adopting rational interpretations under conditions of disturbing emotional feelings will change our behaviour as well as the behaviour of the person who is provoking an emotional feeling in us. (Ellis, A., 2004., 2001., 1994., 1977., 1975.)

Behaviour Modification Therapy:

Personality studies do not have much relevance in the 'Behaviourism' school of thought. Personality traits or behaviour styles are not at the focus of their studies. Research findings of Evan P. Pavlov, J.B. Watson, B.F. Skinner and others are not about personality or personality development, but are on the behavioural processes that affect personality. Changing or modifying behaviour is at their focus and such attempts for modifying behaviour is generally known as 'Behaviour Modification Therapy'.

(Pavlov, I.P. 1927; 2001., Skinner, B.F. 1971., 1965; Watson, J.B. 1919., 2008)

Although psychological approaches and theories are different, it is also true that there are many similarities between them. Personal relationships, social relationships, emotionality such as excitement, fear, courage, and anxiety are all related to happiness and success. An application program built on modern psychological theories alone can achieve the intended results for personal growth and personality development.

Glossary of Terms:

Analytic psychology: The school of thought developed and propagated by Carl Gustav Jung, a Swiss psychiatrist.

Anima: The female side of a male.

Animus: The male side of a female.

Attitude: A mind set or disposition to behave in a predetermined way based of one's past experiences; prejudice or pre-judgements to act without any logical analysis of facts and figures.

Autonomy Vs doubt: Freedom to act or its opposite hesitations/doubt.

Basic anxiety: Karen Horney's assumption of life- insecurity arising out of the birth trauma – i.e. expulsion from the comfort of the womb to an uncertain world.

Behaviour dispositions: Tendency to behave in a particular way as in the case of a trait or a habit.

Behaviour pattern: The profile variations when many traits of a person are listed and described

Behaviour skills and style: The unique pattern of a person when many traits of attributes are listed and described.

Behaviour therapy/Behaviour modifications: Behavioural change based on the principles of learning/unlearning.

Birth order: The birth order position of the child such as the first and the eldest, the last and the youngest, the middle etc.

Cardinal traits: The dominant and prominent traits of a person which are few in number.

Central traits: Common traits applicable to all, but differ in quantitative variations among many.

Collective unconscious: A cultural heritage of mankind in which certain symbols which stand for certain ideas are common to all human beings and which functions at the unconscious levels of each person.

Complexes: Emotionally charged wishes that are repressed when there is a conflict between Id and Ego or between Id and Super Ego or between Ego and Super Ego. Any emotionally charged wish or idea is often called a complex such as inferiority complex, superiority complex etc.

Conflicts: Clash of two or more equally powerful forces or urges within our mind.

Conscious: self awareness of what is happening in the environment of a person on which actions are based.

Creativity: Thinking in a deviant way for appreciation and recognition from others (dependency) Vs exercising one's own freedom to take decisions and actions without caring much on what others may think about it (autonomy).

Dependency Vs Autonomy: Always looking for approval and appreciation (Dependency) Vs. Free from such dependency (Autonomy).

Dreams: Symbolic satisfaction of repressed wishes through dreams at sleep; Self fulfilment wishes.

Death instinct: When libido is directed towards destructive purposes, it is called death instinct.

Ego: The reality orientation fully self conscious that controls and directs human behaviour.

Ego defence mechanisms: Self justification mechanisms resorted to by the ego for protecting the self when certain wishes/urges are repressed.

Ego identity Vs Role confusion: A clear picture of who am I or confusion on one's role in life.

Emotive traits: Motivational and emotional traits such as need for achievements, need for social acceptance, need for power etc.

Eros and Thanatoes: Eros is the life instinct and Thanatoes is the death instinct.

Escape from freedom: The tendency to be a slave for the protection and comforts others provide for the person. Providing too much welfare for nothing in return may make the State rulers authoritarian and totalitarian by subjugating the people.

Exploitative orientation: Taking away from others without their willingness by hook or crook methods.

Extroversion: When the life energy is flowing outside the person and he/she takes interest in external affairs, he/she is known to be an extrovert.

Factor analysis: A statistical method based on inter-correlations among many attributes for identifying the latent common attribute among such diverse attributes.

Family drama: A family consists of parents and their children, the main social environment of a growing child; social interactions of these members within the family system are very significant, according to Alfred Adler.

Functional autonomy: Something that occurred earlier with the perception of cause-effect relations, but now occurs as a habit without the perception of the cause factor; an action that has become self driven, though originally it was not so.

Generitivity Vs stagnation: productive activity or stagnating inactivity.

Hoarding orientation: Being miserly for a better tomorrow and such tomorrows are always postponed.

Humanistic approach: Activities and approaches for the benefits of mankind.

Humanistic communistic socialism: The school of thought propagated by Erich Fromm which was taken up by others as political ideology. M.N. Roy's 'Radical socialism' belongs to this ideology.

Id: Biological and other unconscious wishes of a person which are natural urges without modified and controlled by the reality orientation.

Identification: Identification is the process of assuming that the person himself/herself is the object/hero of the story. Here, identification is self identification.

Individual psychology: The school of thought on personality developed and propagated by Alfred Adler.

Industry Vs Inferiority: Efforts at achieving something or feeling of insignificance on failure to succeed.

Inferiority complex: A sense of inadequacy/insufficiency that results in desirable or undesirable compensatory behaviour.

Initiative Vs guilt: Self initiative success in actions or its opposite feeling of failure/shame.

Integrity Vs Despair: A happy feeling of a meaningful life lived or a feeling that that the bygone life was a meaningless one.

Intimacy Vs Isolation: Close association between two persons to the extent of sharing everything or its other extreme of isolation and avoidance.

Introversion: When the life energy of a person is drawn to the inward self, it is called introversion; a socially withdrawn personality

Emotional stability: a well balanced type personality with less emotional disturbance.

Extroversion/Extraversion: An outgoing sociable type personality.

Libido: According to Sigmund Freud, Libido is the sex energy whereas it is life energy for other philosophers and psychologists.

Life instinct: When the Libido is directed towards constructive purposes, it is called life instinct.

Marketing orientation: Assuming oneself as product to be sold in the market of give and take conditions, depending on the demand and supply positions.

Masculine protest: The tendency to protest and disown one's shortcomings and weaknesses is named as masculine protest on the assumption that males are strong and females are weak.

Mindsets: A frame of reference of the mind to act in a predetermined way depending on his/her past experiences.

Modelling: Learning by observations and imitations.

Motivation: The psychological energy and force that generates and directs the behaviour of a person.

Moving against: Others are there to harm the person and the belief that the best strategy to protect self is to move against them i.e. 'attack them before they attack me'.

Moving away: The strategy adopted by a person of being self sufficient and independent to avoid the problems created by others.

Moving towards: Getting a feeling of security and comfort in the presence of others as if that the others will protect if one moves towards them.

Moving with: Smooth and cordial relationship with others on mutual acceptance and co-operations.

Neuroticism: Emotionally disturbed type behaviour patterns.

Persona: Common symbolic ideas of desirable social presentations of individuals; a social mask for a desirable self presentation.

Personal growth Vs personality development: Growth is the natural unfolding of potentials and development is the deliberate nurturing of skills, competence and capabilities.

Personal unconscious: Personal unconscious are experiences of a person that are repressed (complex) that create behavioural pathologies subsequently.

Personality: The behaviour pattern and behaviour dispositions that create the individuality or uniqueness of a person.

Personality traits: Behaviour dispositions or a group of behaviour activities that are consistent and well integrated.

Personology: Comprehensive study of a person as a psycho-social being.

Preconscious: Awareness of things and events at the periphery of attention, not at the focus; somewhat half conscious of things, not the details.

Productive orientation: Positive and constructive activities for the expressions of one's competence and talents; realization of self actualization.

Projection: One of the defence mechanisms wherein the person tries to defend himself/herself from undesirable thoughts and feelings by externalizing them into others. This externalization is called projection.

Psychoanalysis: The school of thought on mind initiated and established by Sigmund Freud.

Psychodynamics: Conscious and unconscious psychological energies and forces that cause behaviour of an individual.

Psychopathology of everyday life: Aberrational behaviour that gives expression to the repressed unconscious urges such as slip of the tongue, obsessive thoughts, compulsive acts etc.

Psychosexual development: There are six stages of development in one's life span; they are, oral pleasure, anal pleasure, and latent stage, and phallic stage, homosexual and heterosexual stage.

psychosocial development: The theory in which Erik Erikson elaborates eight stages of development viz., Trust Vs mistrust; Autonomy Vs shame/doubt; Initiative Vs Guilt; Industry Vs inferiority; Ego identity Vs Role confusion; Intimacy Vs isolation; Generativity Vs stagnation; integrity Vs despair.

Psychoticism: An extreme case of mental disorder wherein time and space orientations of the patient are lost for a short period or longer periods.

REBT: Abbreviation for Rational Emotive Behaviour Therapy. i.e. a system of behaviour modification by new interpretation of a situation for changing the emotional tone associated with the interpretations.

Rationalization: Rationalization is one of the defence mechanisms wherein the person tries to justify all his/her actions/expressions, inspite of their perceived irrationality by others.

Receptive frame of orientation: Receiving/Accepting everything from others without any reciprocity.

Relatedness: Social associations among people; interpersonal relations.

Repression: Banishment of a socialy undesirable wish that becomes weak by our inner conflicts and which subsequently becomes unconscious complex; such complexes create mental problems for the person.

Rootedness: Impact of the earliest associations and relationship within a community that affect his/her behaviour.

Secondary traits: Unimportant and less significant traits.

Self: One' own picture about oneself that a person has.

Self actualization: Explicit expressions of one's own talents and other capabilities.

Self concept: An image about self as experienced by the person.

Self efficacy: The belief system of a person that he/she is capable of achieving the desired results.

Shadow: An archetype of undesirable negative picture of the self.

Sixteen (16) PF: Sixteen source traits (personality factors) as given by R.B. Cattell.

Social cognition theory: The theory put forward by Albert Bandura wherein learning takes place by observations and imitations.

Source traits: Latent common factor traits among many surface level personality attributes found by the statistical technique of 'Factor Analysis'.

Subconscious: Anything that is not at the conscious level— a general term for unconscious and preconscious together.

Superego: The moral and ethical constraints on behaviour imposed by the teachings of parents, teachers and neighbours during the early childhood period and which acts as an unconscious force on our behaviour.

Suppression: Conscious banishment of a wish when it is a socially undesirable one in our inner conflicts which we are aware of; a painful experience that we are aware of but no further complication is created by such mechanism.

Surface traits: Visible behaviour activities or cluster of activities exhibited by a person.

Traits Vs types: Traits are specific behaviour dispositions whereas types are higher order level groupings of traits. i.e., clustering a number of traits forms the type.

Trust/mistrust: Acceptance of/positive approach to others or its counterpart, rejection/ avoidance.

Unconscious: When a person is aware of the effect, but not aware of its cause, it is said to be unconscious.

References:

Adler, Alfred. (1964).

Superiority and social Interest: a collection of Later Writings.

NY: W.W. Norton & Co.

Adler, A. (1959)

Practice and theory of Individual Psychology.

NJ: Littlefield, Adams.

Adler, A. (1957).,

Understanding Human Nature.

NY: Premier Books.

Allport, G.W. (1961).,

Pattern and Growth in Personality.

NY: Holt, Rinehart &Winston.

Allport, G.W. (1937).,

Personality: A Psychological Interpretation.

NY: Holt, Rinehart and Winston.

Bandura, Albert, 1997

Self Efficacy: the Exercise of Control.

NY: W.H. Freeman.

Bandura, Albert. 1977.

Social learning Theory.

NJ: Prentice Hall.

Bandura, albert, 1969.

Principles of Behaviour Modifications.

NY: Holt, Rinehart & Winston.

Cattell, R.B. 1952.,

Factor Analysis: An Introduction and Manual for the Psychologist and social scientist.

NY: Harper & Row.

Cattell, R.B., 1946.

The description and Measurement of Personality.

NY: Harcourt, Brace & World.

Ellis, A., 2004,

Rational Emotive Behaviour Therapy: It Works for Me – It Can Work for You.

NY: Prometheus Books.

Ellis, A., 2001.

Feeling Better, Getting Better, Staying Better: Profound Self Help therapy for Your Emotions.

California: Impact Publishers.

Ellis, A., 1994.

Reason and Emotion in Psychotherapy.

NJ: Carol Publishing Group.

Ellis, A., 1977.

Handbook of Rational Emotive Therapy.

NY: Springer Publishing.

Ellis, A., 1975.

A New Guide to Rational living.

California: Wilshire Book Company.

Erik Erikson. (1968)

Identity: Youth and Crisis.

NY: W.W. Norton & Co.

Erik Erikson. (1950)

Childhood and Society.

NY: W.W. Norton & Co.

Eysenck, H.J. (1960).,

The Structure of Human Personality.

London: Methuen.

Eysenck, H.J., (1959).,

Maundslay Personality Inventory.

London: University of London Press.

Eysenck, H.J. (1947).,

Dimensions of Personality.

London: Routledge.

Freud, S. (1990).,

New Introductory Lectures on Psychoanalysis.

NY: Norton, 1933.

NY: W.W. Norton &Company.

Freud, S. (2011).,

The Ego and the Id.

Connecticut: Martino Fine Books.

Freud, S. (1977).,

Introductory Lectures on Psychoanalysis.

NY: W.W. Norton and company.

Freud, S. (1962)

Three Contributions to the Theory of Sex.

NY: Dutton.

Freud, S. (2021).,

The Psychopathology of Every Day Life.

India: Fingerprint publishing.

Freud, S. (2019)

The Interpretation of Dreams.

New Delhi: Om Books International.

Fromm, Erich. (2005)

To Have or To Be.

London: Continuum Publishers.

Fromm, Erich. (1990).,

The Sane Society.

NY: Henry Holt.

Fromm, Erich. (1941)

Escape From Freedom.

NY: Henry Holt.

Horney, K. (1945)

Our Inner conflicts.

NY; W.W. Norton.

Horney, K. (1942)

Self Analysis.

NY: Norton & Co.

Horney, K. (1950).,

The Neurotic Personality of Our Time.

Original first publication, (1937)

NY: W.W. Norton.

Jung, C.G. (1964)

Man and his Symbols.

NY: Doubleday.

Jung, C.G. (1959)

The archetypes and the collective Unconscious.

Collected Works of C.G. Jung, Vol. 16.

New Jersey: Princeton University Press

Jung, C.G. (1933).,

Psychological types.

NY: Harcourt, Brace &World.

Jung, C.G. (1925).,

Psychology of the Unconscious.

NY: Dodd, Mead.

Maslow, A.H., (1954)

Motivation and Personality.

NY: Harper &Row.

Murray, H. A. (1938).,

Explorations in Personality.

NY: Oxford University Press.

Rogers, C.R. (1961)

On Becoming a Person: A Therapist's View of Psychotherapy.

Boston: Houghton Mifflin.

Rogers, C.R. (1951)

Client Centred Therapy: Its Current Practice, Implications and Theory.

Boston: Houghton and Mifflin.

Pavlov, I.P. (1927).,

Conditioned Reflexes: An Investigation of the Physiological Activity of the Cerebral Cortex.

London: Oxford University Press.

Pavlov, I. P (2001)

Selected Works,

London: Oxford University Press.

Skinner, B.F. (1971)

Beyond Freedom and dignity.

Indianapolis: Hackett Publishing Co.

Skinner, B.F. 1965.

Science and Human behaviour.

California: Free Press.

Watson, J.B. (2008)

Behaviourism.

Minnesota: WEST Press.

Watson, J.B. (1919)

Psychology from the Standpoint of a behaviourist.

Philadelphia: Lippincott.

Chapter 3

Positive Psychology

1879 is a milestone in the history of psychology. The first psychology laboratory in the world was established at the University of Leipzig in Germany in the year 1879. It was established by Wilhelm Wundt, a German philosopher. What part of the body is the mind? Is it the functioning of the sensory organs that give us knowledge of the world? Wundt developed a system of studying the physical and physiological processes that give rise to experiences through the senses. It was the beginning of psychophysics, and physiological/biological psychology. Here begins the historical truth that transformed philosophical psychology into a science of psychology. According to Wilhelm Wundt, Psychology was the study of the subjective experience of consciousness (Wundt, W. 1897). This definition of psychology continued for a long time, till Sigmund Freud dethroned it by his 'discovery' of the unconscious. The psychological studies of Wundt and his associates are known as the structural school of thought in psychology. The school of thought popularised by Freud is known as the Psychoanalytic school.

Studies of the structural parts of personal experiences of a person are important, no doubt. But, its functions that help the person to adjust well to the demands of his/her environment is more important in psychology. This view was advocated by pragmatic functionalists William James and John Dewey (James, W. 1981., 2015; Dewy, J. 1925). Their way of thinking was called the functional school of psychology.

Ivan P. Pavlov's discovery of 'conditioned reflex' as the core concept of 'learning' was the foundation of 'Behaviorism' advocated by John B. Watson, and B.F. Skinner. According to these behaviourists, objective methods to study observable behaviour of a person, is to be at the focus of psychology. This school of thought in Psychology is called the school of Behaviourism. The visible overt behaviour and the internal covert behaviour are equally important, but, the not visible internal thoughts, feelings, emotions etc., are to be made visible by an operational definition of such concept, according to these behaviourists (Pavlov, I.P. 2003 Skinner, B.F. 1953; Watson, J.B. 2010).

Different Schools of thought in Psychology:

The main difference between modern psychology and philosophical thoughts on mind is the methodology of studying the subject. Philosophical thoughts are based on logic and experience; Modern psychology, on the other hand is based on empirical evidences based on observations and experimentations. A landmark in the history of psychology was the establishment of a laboratory in 1879 by Wilhem Wundth at the University of Leipzig, Germany. Thereafter, there have been many schools of thought in psychology. -- Structural, Functional, Analytical, Gestalt or integrative, Behavioural etc.

The proponents of Structural psychology were Wilhelm Wundt (1896) and Edward B. Titchener (2007) who stressed the importance of the anatomy of subjective experiences for the understanding of consciousness. Structuralism defined psychology as the study of consciousness or subjective experiences.

The philosopher psychologist, William James and educationist John Dewy with their stress on American pragmatism, stressed the relevance of the usefulness of behaviour and their school of thought is known as Functionalism in psychology. Better adjustment to the demands of the environment was their stress.

Sigmund Freud, (1990; 1953) a neurologist turned psychologist and his followers were of the view that mental diseases are the products of conflicts and repressions in the psychodynamic process. This school of thought is known as Psychoanalysis. Variations from psychoanalysis, such as Individual psychology of Alfred Adler, Analytic psychology of C.G, Jung and other forms by the neo Freudians are more philosophical than empirical. Karen Horney and Eric Fromm are noteworthy authors among the neo-Freudians.

As a counter force to this analytical approach in understanding the mind, Wertheimer (1981), Kohler (1981) and other German psychologists emphasised the need for looking at the totality of the behavioural situations for a better understanding. This approach is known as the gestalt school of thought. Meaningful integration is equally important as the analytical approach that identifies the elements of the 'whole' as a phenomenon.

What can be observed by an outsider in terms of muscular movements, facial expressions, languages etc are to be stressed in understanding behaviour, without diluting the relevance of covert behaviour of emotions, feeling, images, thoughts etc The emphasis on overt behaviour and understanding of the internal mental processes are to be subjected to experimentations by operational definitions of the mental concept. John B. Watson, and B.F. Skinner were the pioneers in this school of thought known as Behaviourism.

Positive Psychology

At the forefront of such schools right now is the school of thought known as positive psychology. The idea that psychology should be the knowledge needed for human success and happiness is echoed in this school of thought. Instead of 'what', 'why' and 'how' of mental illnesses, the main topic of discussion should be on the characteristics of mental health in a positive way and not on mental diseases. The focus of positive psychology is on this condition of mental health aspect. A psychologist Dr. Martin Seligman is the originator and developer of this line of thoughts in modern psychology. In his presidential address to the American Psychology Association in the year 1998, Dr. Seligman stressed the importance of positive psychology of mental health and happiness.

What is Positive Psychology?

Sociologist Auguste Comte (2021) elaborated the 'positivism' approach in social sciences as a non evaluative description of the observed phenomenon. 'Positivism' describes the approach that does not fall under the classification of 'good' or 'bad' facts under observations. The knowledge that leads to a good desirable life is described as 'normative', not 'positive'. The focus of normative approach is on 'what should be or what ought to be' from the standards of the society. Positive psychology does approve the normative approach rather than the positivism. The normative approach of the positive psychologists emphasised the need to study the positive mental health rather than the negative approach focussing on mental illness or behaviour pathologies. That is, the approach that psychology should adopt should be conducive for a happy and successful life. Although the science of psychology has embraced positivism, positive psychology is normative for leading a better life – not understanding and treating mental diseases, but understanding the psychology that leads to a happy and successful life.

Positive psychology is a science that analyzes in detail what are the psychological factors that lead to 'psychological wellbeing'. Positive psychology is a science that explains the psychological principles behind happiness and success in life. Brief notes on the psychologists who gave direction to positive psychology and explained the principles behind the psychological wellness, are given below.

Dr. Seligman, M.P.E:

Dr. Martin Seligman is considered as the founder, developer and strong advocate of positive psychology. He defined positive psychology as the scientific study of human strengths and virtues that lead to a happy and successful life of individuals, communities and organizations (Seligman, M.P.E. 2002., 2004., 2006., 2011). According to Seligman, there are three types of happiness: A pleasant life, a good life and a meaningful life. Life is to enjoy by satisfaction of sensory cravings is the motto of the pleasant life; A life that is smooth without an unpleasant traumatic experiences is called a good life; The feeling that my life has been meaningful in terms of contributing something for the benefits to others is the real meaningful life.

Concepts and theories contributed by Dr. Seligman are as follows:

1. Life experiences are to be pleasant emotions to avoid a pessimistic orientation in life. Seligman calls this as 'learnt optimism' (Seligman, M.P.E, 1991)

2. The happiness that you experience is to be a sustained one for a long period and not a temporary pleasure by taking food, drinks etc. The concept that he uses for this kind of pleasant experience is 'Authentic Happiness' (Seligman, 2002)

3. 'Flourish' is another concept for sustained happiness with PERMA model--- Pleasant emotions, Engagements, Relationships, Meaningfulness and Accomplishment. (Seligman, 2011)

4. 24 character strengths and virtues are discussed for the understanding of human flourishing (Seligman, MPE and Peterson, C. 2004)

5. Scientific and practical explorations of human strengths and virtues and ways and means of overcoming factors that are hindrances to sustained happiness (Seligman and Mihaly Csikantzmihali, 2008).

Dr. Mihaly Csikszentmihalyi:

The concept 'Flow' was the main contribution to positive psychology by Dr. Mihaly Csikszantmihali. 'Flow' is described as a state of optimal experience wherein the person is fully involved and immersed in the meaningful activity he/she is engaged. Feeling of timelessness, deep focus, enjoyment, increased productivity, a sense of wellbeing and an overall satisfaction are the main characteristics of 'Flow'. Dr. Mihaly did not ignore the existence of mental disorders and dysfunctions, but emphasised the need for positive side of human experience: happiness, wellbeing, resilience and fulfilment. His extensive research works were on the applications of the flow theory to education, business and sports, especially on the relevance of creativity and inventions (Mihaly, Csikszantmihalyi, 2003., 2004., 2008., 1998).

Dr. Ed Diener:

Edward Diener, also known as Ed. Diener is another person worth mentioning among the significant contributors of positive psychology. He had studied in detail the concept of Subjective Well-Being (SWB.)

and its relevance to happiness and success in life. His scientific measurement of SWB and studies on cross cultural differences are worth mentioning. The need for a national index on happiness/SWB was also stressed by ED Diener. Because of his contribution to the phenomenon of happiness, others often addressed him as Doctor Happiness.

Some of his interesting findings are: (1) One in three people in the USA are happy. (2) Up to a certain point, wealth and happiness are correlated, but beyond a critical point, no such correlation exists. Psychological wealth is not financial prosperity; it is the subjective feeling of well-being. (Ed Diener, 2009., 2008., 2003)

Dr. Mary Jahoda:

Mary Jahoda's research findings are important components of positive psychology -- although she is best known as a social psychologist. According to her, the absence of mental illness should not be taken as a sign of mental health. Signs of positive mental health are: (1) Positive attitude towards oneself. (2) Self-actualization. (3) Harmony/ Integration. (4) Self-reliance/Autonomy. (5) Perception of reality. (6) Ability to influence and control one's own environment.

A social mind to work cooperatively with others and the ability to manage time efficiently are also signs of mental health. Current concept of positive mental health (Jahoda, M., 1958), also deals how unemployment affects mental health (Jahoda, M., 1982) and the social aspect of health, illness and healthcare (Jahoda, M., 1998.

Dr. Barbara Fredrickson:

Another well-known figure in positive psychology is Barbara Frederickson. Her contributions include research findings on the positive emotions of love, joy, pride, and motivation. Love is not a feeling but a social relationship. Positive emotions include feelings of connectedness, gratitude, and personal actions for the good of others. (Barbara Fredrickson., 2018., 2009., 2004).

Dr. Ellen Langer:

Harvard professor Ellen Langer's main research focused on mindfulness, happy living, and ageing. She took 40 people over 70 years of age and divided them into two groups; 20 of them as an experimental group and the other 20 as control groups. The experimental group was subjected to the practice of mindfulness and repeated their lifestyle at 20s.

This experiment started in 1979. After the completion of the experiment, the two groups were compared on certain specified behavioural dimensions (for meaningful comparison the experimental and controlled groups were subjected to the same behavioural before and after the experiment.); at the final stage of comparison, most of the control group members behaved like 70-year-old year; Most of the experimental group members exhibited a life style of their 50 years. The observed difference was found significant to warrant meaningful generalizations. The answer to the question of 'how old are you' depends on how young is your mind, in spite of your chronological age. (Langer, Ellan., 2010., 1989).

Following are the key principles that summarize the descriptions and conclusions of positive psychology researchers:

1. Arrange your interpersonal and social relationships to the liking of others.

2. Work for the benefits of others. Those who do social services are generally cheerful and happy.

3. Understand the meaning of work and leisure activities. It is not a job for a salary that matters, but a salary for a given job.

4. Implement lifestyle habits to foster mindfulness, positive thinking, and happiness.

5. Demonstrate a joyful flow in all activities. Don't waste opportunities to show your talents and skills.

6. Physical health is also important.

7. When we talk about the need for attention and empowerment in one's actions, the words of the 'Bhagavad Gita' come to my mind: Karma (Engagement) is your duty; Don't do karma to get desired results; the result will depend on the nature of karma; everything in your life is the result of your karma.

Glossary of Terms:

Accomplishment: Achieving the set goals.

Achievement: A feeling of efficacy that one experiences on reaching the set goals.

Authentic Happiness: Genuine sustained happiness that lasts for a long period.

Behaviouristic Psychology: Observable overt behaviour and unobservable mental processes, the presence of which can be made overt by operational definitions of the concepts and/or, constructs are at the focus of the behaviourists, Ivan P, Pavlov, John B. Watson, B.F. Skinner and others.

Character strengths and virtues: Psychological traits or behaviour dispositions that foster positive emotions conducive to success and happiness.

Creativity: The process of looking at familiar things as strange and then making such strange things familiar.

Deep Focus: sustained deep attention to something for a period banishing other thoughts and feelings.

Discovery: Finding out something as new, different from the existing ones.

Engagement: Involvement and participation in an activity; if it is for monitory compensation, it is an employment or work; if it is for its own sake without expecting a reward, then it is a hobby or a leisure time activity.

Enjoyment: Strong pleasant feeling for a short period.

Flourish: Psychological factors associated with the blossoming of happiness, wellbeing and success

Flow: A state of optimal experience wherein the person is fully involved and immersed in his engagement.

Fulfilment: Meaningful attainment of a purpose

Functional Psychology: study of behaviour/mind with focus on its usefulness for better adjustment to the demands of the environment; a pragmatic approach in psychology advocated by William James, John Dewy and others.

Gestalt Psychology: A School of thought that emphasised the need for considering the wholeness of the situations and the need for integrating parts of the wholeness. This School of thought was advocated by German psychologists Wertheimer, Kohler and others.

Good Life: A smooth life without anxiety, worry, fear etc.

Happiness: A feeling of wellness and satisfaction in life, with sustained pleasant feelings, irrespective of favourable or unfavourable life circumstances.

Inventions: creating something new for practical purposes such as instruments, machine, methods, procedure etc.

Learned Optimism: The product of acquisition of positive emotions by self efforts.

Meaningful Life: A sense of attaining the purpose of being useful and helpful by an engagement.

Meaningfulness: clarity of purpose in doing something and the purpose that one likes.

Optimal experience: Optimal means neither less nor more; the right quality and quantity of experience.

Overall Satisfaction: Sustained feeling of satisfaction that lingers for a longer period.

PERMA: P is for Positive emotions; E is for Engagement; R is for Relationships; M is for Meaningfulness and A is for Accomplishment

Pleasant Emotions: Feelings and emotions such as satisfaction, pleasure, joy, soothing excitement etc opposed to anxiety, worry, fear, anger etc.

Pleasant Life: Experiencing pleasure by consumptions and sensory excitement.

Positive Psychology: study of human success and happiness by explorations of human mind advocated by Martin Seligman and his associates.

Positivism: Pure narrations of an event or phenomenon without any evaluative judgements using subjective criteria.

Productivity: Efficiency in engagement and performance by investment of less time, less efforts and optimal use of resources. Productivity is a ratio wherein the output is more than the input.

Relationships: Interpersonal and social relationships. It could be friendship relations, family relations, business relations etc.

Resilience: The power or ability to return to the normal conditions in adverse circumstances

Positive Psychology: study of human success and happiness by explorations of human mind advocated by Martin Seligman and his associates.

Psychoanalytic Psychology: Study of the unconscious dynamic factors that influence behaviour advocated by Sigmund Freud and his followers.

Structural Psychology: Study of the components of conscious experiences advocated by Wilhelm Wundt and his associates.

Timelessness: Unaware of the time taken by deep involvement in an engagement.

Wellbeing: A human condition of success, happiness and wellness.

Wellness: A life condition opposite to illness; a healthy condition rather than a condition of physical and mental disorders.

References:

Comte, Auguste. (2021).,

A General View of Positivism., Or summary Exposition of the System of Thought and Life.

Penguin Group U.S.A.: Alpha Edition (Paperback).

Dewy, John. (1925)

Experience and Nature,

NY: Dover Publications, Inc.

Diener, Ed. (2009)

Well-Being for Public Policy. (Oxford Positive Psycholgy Series.).

U.K.: Oxford University Press.

Ed Diener and Diener, R.B. (2008).

Happiness: Unlocking of the mysteries of Psychological Wealth.

New Jersy: Wiley-Blackwell,

Ed Diener, et. al. (2003).

Well-Being: Foundations of Hedonic Psychology.

NY: Russell Sage Foundation,

Fredrickson, Barbara., Et. al. (2018).,

Positive Emotions and Optimal Health

U.K.: Oxford University Press.

Fredrickson, Barbara. (2009).,

Positivity: Top Notch Research Reveals the Upward Spiral That Will Change Your Life.

California: Harmony.

Fredrickson, Barbara., et. al (2004)

The Psychology of Gratitude.

U.K.: Oxford University Press.

Freud, S. (1953)

A General Introduction to Psychoanalysis.

NY: Doubleday.

Freud, S., (1990).

New Introductory Lectures on Psychoanalysis.

NY: W.W. Norton &Company.

James, William. (1981)

Pragmatism: A New Name for Some Old Ways of Thinking.

Indianapolis: Hackett Publishing Co.

James, William. (2015)

The Principles of Psychology

California: Createspace Independent Publishing Platform.

Jahoda, Marie. (1982)

Employment and Unemployment: A Social- Psychological Analysis: 1 (The Psychology of Social Issues)

U.K.: Cambridge University Press.

Jahoda, Marie. (1979).,

Current Concept of Positive Mental Health.

U.K.: Iyer Company Publishing Inc.

Kohler, W. (1981)

Dynamic in Psychology: Vital Applications of Gestalt Psychology.

NY: Liveright, Revised Edn.

Langer, Ellen. (2010).,

Counter Clockwise: A Proven Way to Think Yourself Younger and Healthier.

NY: Hodder (Paperbacks).

Langer, Ellen. (1989).,

Mindfulness.

Boston: Addison-Wesley.

Mihaly, Csikszantmihalyi (2013)

Creativity: The Psychology of Discovery and Inventions.

NY: Harper Perennial.

Mihaly, Csikszentmihalyi. (2008).,

Flow: The Psychology of Optimal Experience.

NY: Harper Perennial Modern Classics.

Mihaly, Csikszantmihalyi., (2004)

Good Business: Leadership, Flow, and the Making of meaning.

London: Penguin Books.

Mihaly, Csikszantmihalyi. (1998).,

Finding Flow: The Psychology of Engagement with Every Day Life.

NY: Basic Books.

Pavlov, I.P. (2003)

Lectures on conditioned Reflexes.

NY: Dover Publications.

Saligman, M.P.E. (2011).,

Flourish: A Visionary New Understanding of happiness and Wellbeing.

NY: Atria Books.

Seligman, M.P.E. (2006)

Learned Optimism: How to Change Your Mind and Your Life.

NY: Vintage Books.

Seligman, M.P.E. and Peterson, Christopher. (2004).,

Character Strengths and Virtues: A Handbook and Classifications.

U.K.: Oxford University Press.

Seligman, M.P.E. (2004).,

Authentic Happiness: Using the New Positive Psychology to Realize Your Potential for Lasting Fulfilment.

NY: Atria Books.

Seligman, M.P.E. and Mihaly Csikszentmihalyi. (2000).,

Positive Psychology: The Scientific and Practical Exploration of Human Strengths.

U.S.A.: American Psychology Association.

Skinner, J.F. (1953)

Science and Human Behaviour

NY: Macmillan.

Titchner, E.B. (2007).,

A Text Book of Psychology.,

USA: Kissinger, Pub. Co.

Watson, J.B. (2010).,

Psychology From the Standpoint of a Behaviourist.,

USA: Kessinger Publishing.

Wertheimer. (1981).,

Dynamics in Psychology: Vital Applications of Gestalt Psychology.

NY: Liverright, Revised Edition.

Wunt, Wilhelm, (1896).,

Outlines of Psychology.,

Engelmann, Leipzig.

Chapter 4

Psychometric Tests for the Measurement of Psychological Attributes

What is measurement and how it is measured?

"If anything exists, it exists in amount and it can be measured" This often repeated quotation is attributed to Edward L. Thorndike, a well known educational psychologist. Though there is no direct reference to this quotation in any one of his works, others attributed this quotation to him because of his contributions on measurement of psychological traits and educational achievements.

Quantification in numbers of an attribute or variable is the essence of measurement (Kaplan, D. et. al. 2009) The qualitative attribute of a term is connotation and the quantitative extensiveness of the term is the concept of denotation. Connotation is concerned with quality and denotation is concerned with quantity. In formal logic, the denotation is often expressed in the term of 'all', 'none', 'some' and 'some not' expressions.

Does an attribute exist or not? The value of existence is 1 and the value of non-existence is 0. If the value is 1 and one alone, then it is an attribute of a nominal type and if the value goes beyond 1 i.e. 1,2,3,4,...n etc., then it is a variable. If it is only an attribute and not a variable, then the measurement is only a label for counting. How many People are there wearing red shirts? The answer is in terms of counting and there is no variable of red shirts. Labelling and counting the items is the essence of nominal scales.

Another scale is for the measurement of relative positions of an attribute (ordinal scale). Maintaining equal distance from one point to the next adjacent point is the interval scale and an interval scale with an absolute zero point for higher level mathematical operations is known as the Ratio scale (Allen J.M. 2004; DeVellis, R.F. 2016; James, R.M/ et. al. 2018).

A scale is an instrument for measurement. There are different categories of scales as described below:

1. **Nominal Scale:** Assigning a number or a name for identification is the essence of nominal scale. This labelling may help us for categorization/ classification. The relative position of each number is not known in nominal scales. Possible mathematical operations in nominal scale are: Frequency counts; Mode; contingency tables; Chi-square; cluster analysis; Categorical analysis; Bar/Pie charts etc.

2. **Ordinal Scale:** When the numbers are arranged in ascending or descending order, we may say an 'x' number is above or below a 'y' number. This order of greater than or lesser than, is the essence of an ordinal scale. Comparison is possible in an ordinal scale, but, Mathematical operations are limited to ranking, ordinal comparison, Mode, and Percentile, nonparametric tests such as Spearman's Rank order correlation, Categorical analysis etc. are possible under the ordinal scale. Higher levels of mathematical operations are not possible in the ordinal scale for, there are no equal intervals between adjacent numbers and no absolute or arbitrary zero point.

3. **Interval Scale:** An ordinal scale with equal distance of adjacent scale values is known as the interval scale, but without an absolute starting point of zero. The starting point could be an arbitrary one such as the freezing point of water at the lower level and the boiling point of water at the upper terminal level.

4. **The Ratio Scale:** The ideal and the most useful scale is the ratio scale wherein all types of mathematical operations are possible. A ratio scale is an interval scale with an absolute zero point. Physical attributes such as length, width, height, weight etc., are usually measured by ratio scales.

The relationship between quality and quantity:

Anything that exists without quantitative variations is an attribute and an attribute with quantitative variation is a variable. If an attribute without quantitative variation is an abstract conceptual idea, then, quantification of that quality is possible by an operational definition of the concept. Time and space are most abstract concepts, yet we are in a position to measure them by some tangible observations such as the length of our shadow when the sun is bright or the position of a star, or mechanical movement of a needle in some instruments. So conversion of an intangible quality is possible by some operational definition of the attribute. Similarly, a quantitative variable may be converted into a qualitative category by arbitrary classification such as age variable conversion into Infants, boys, adolescents, adults etc. (Kaplan, D. et/al. 2009.

The Mindset/Personality:

Difference between behavioural traits that are observed by others and traits that are not directly visible to others is explained below: visible and observable behaviour attributes are called behaviour or behaviour patterns and the disposition to behave that predicts possible actual behaviour is called behaviour traits or mind sets. Personality traits are not observed behaviour or behaviour pattern, but, a prediction of possible behaviour or behaviour patterns by the observations of disposition or mind set. A habit is an actual behaviour whereas a trait is only a prediction of possible behaviour or behaviour patterns. (Allport, G.W. 1927., 1961; Bischoff L.J. 1970., Cattell, R.B. 1965; Eysenck, H.J. 1998; Marston, V.M. 1979; Oliver P.J. et. al. 2008).

G.W. AllPort's Method of Structural Analysis of personality traits:

There is an endless variety of words in a dictionary on behavioural attributes called traits. G. W. Allport counted such words from the dictionary and removed all synonyms and antonyms and then classified them into physical, physiological and mental traits. This process of reduction of many traits into reduced numbers on the basis of correlations among them is the essence of 'Factor Analysis' as a statistical method. The structural analysis for the reduction of traits by Allport is a forerunner of factor analysis. Later, RB Catell, H.J. Eysenck and others adopted Factor analysis as a method for arriving at the basic structure of personality. (Allport, G.W. 1961; Joe-Omkin and Mueller, C.R. 1978; Cattell, R.B. 1965; Eysenck, H.J. 1998).

Psychological Assessment of Personality/Personal Qualities of a Person:

Can the qualities of the mind be measured? To get the answer to this question, we have to clarify what the 'Mind' is and without such clarification one cannot measure it. If the mind is something that can be observed and experimented by external manifestation of behaviour, then we can measure the mind. The internal processes of thoughts and feelings cannot be observed and as such we may make a logical inference about them by some operational definitions of such processes or behavioural qualities. (Aiken, 2012., Cohen, and Swardlik, 2017., Gregory, 2013., Oliver, 2008., Urbina, 2014., Kohen, 2017)

There are three ways for assessment of the personal qualities of a person:

1. Observation of actual behaviour by a group of observers/ judges: Give an opportunity to the person to exhibit the required quality and observe and record such observation in quantitative form. Interview, Group Discussion, and other situational tests examples for such observation of exhibited behaviour wherein the observers record the quantitative aspects by a rating scale. Agreement among the observers in the form of positive correlations among the ratings by the observers is an indication of the reliability and checking the observations with some known criterion is the measurement of the validity.

2. Projective tests: When we respond to an unstructured or semi-structured or even a structured situation such as a set of inkblots or a set of structured/semi-structured/unstructured pictures,

we tend to project our own thoughts and feelings in our responses. There will be more common agreement among the respondents when the situation is structured; it is likely to be less and less common and more and more unique and individualistic with semi-structured and unstructured situations. The commonality of responses by a person to a set of 10 to 12 pictures or inkblots indicates something unique in that person. The real problem with such projective tests is the interpretation of the responses. We need the help of experts who themselves differ in the interpretations making the method less reliable and valid.

3. Standardized psychometric tests known as personality inventories: In this method, the respondents are requested to agree or disagree or state true or false to a series of statements, intended to measure a particular behavioural quality or attribute or a set of such qualities. When many attributes are measured by the same inventory, it is called a multi-phasic instrument. There is objectivity in the administration and interpretations of the instrument as the same procedure and interpretations by all who handle the test. One has to follow certain procedure for making the test reliable, valid and useful. (Furr, R.M. and Bacharach, V.R. 2013; Price, L.R. 2017; Carter, Philip. 2008; Eysenck, H.J. 1998; Urbina, S. 2014;).

Step by step procedure for the construction of a psychometric test is given below:

1. Clarify the qualitative attribute by an operational definition of the concept.

2. Collect a large number of sample statements that reflect the measurement of the psychological attributed/disposition/trait mentioned under item (1) above.

3. Reject a large number of sample items based on poor discrimination values and ambiguities in the statements.

4. Administer the reduced statements to a large number of individuals of an intended segment with due considerations for gender, age, educational background etc.

5. Make a statistical analysis of the responses given by the subjects in terms of endorsement to the statements. The distribution of the scores obtained by the subjects will provide the standards for the interpretations of the score into poor (below 20th percentile), below average (between 20th and 40th percentile), Average (between 40th and 60th percentile) Above average (between 60th and 80th percentile) and superior (above 80th percentile). If necessary, the average may be further subdivided into Average minus (between 40th and 46th percentile), Average (between 47th and 54th percentile and Average plus (between 55th and 60th percentile). This procedure is called 'standardization' of the test scores.

6. Check the reliability or consistency of responses by finding out the correlations between the test scores of the same individuals on two occasions without much time gap. This method is called test-retest method. Working out correlations of two sections of the test (Odd items as one section and even items as the second section). This method is called the split half method. Another method is creation of two tests for the measurement of the same attribute and finding out the correlation between the two. This method is called 'Equivalent Form method'.

7. Check the validity of the test by finding out the correlation between the test findings and an accepted external criteria such as rating on the attribute by those who had the opportunity to observe the concerned individuals such as teachers, immediate boss, close friends etc. The validity index in the form of a correlation is a check on the original concept of the attribute mentioned under item (1) above.

The psychological test could be a general mental ability test/ intelligence test/ Achievement test/ Aptitude test/ interest test/ Attitude test/personality test. There could be a difference in the administration of the test to Individuals or Group. Difference could also be in the form of paper-pencil test or performance test. (Carter, Philip. 2008; Furr, R.M. and Bucharach, V.R. 2013; Gregory, R.J. 2013; Price, L.R. 2017)

Uses of psychometric tests:

Psychometric tests are used for three main purposes.

1. As a psychiatric diagnostic aid.

2. To measure the ability/competence of candidates for their selection to various positions.

3. As an aid in training individuals for their success in life.

The Psychometric tests are useful in three areas:

1. Clinical psychology.

2. industrial/management psychology

3. Educational psychology.

There are many tests used in clinical psychology. The usefulness of such tests depends on the attitudes of psychiatrists who are basically medical men. Clinical psychologists are only supporters of psychiatrists for treatment of mental illness, though they can act as counsellors and trainers for the maintenance of mental health by proper use of reliable and valid psychometric tools. The use of such tests for job selection depends on the attitude of the human resource managers in the business/industry level. Although the use of psychological tests for training for success in life is tremendous, it has not become very popular today, and in due course it is likely to be very useful and popular.

Popular and known psychometric tests in the market:

1. **Minnesota Multiphasic Personality Inventory (MMPI):**

   Comprehensive description of MMPI is given in chapter 5 and so, only the title is given in this section.

2. **California psychological Inventory (CPI):**

   This popular test is the contribution of Harris G. Gough and Pamela Bradley. In this test, there are 434 items (statements) of which 200 items are taken from the MMPI. The main purpose of MMPI is diagnosis of mental maladjustment, and the CPI aims at identification of personality traits of normal human adults: personality traits such as sociability, Empathy, tolerance, Dominance, maturity, Responsibility, Intellectual Efficiency etc,. Those who are within the age group of 12-70 years, both male and female, are eligible for taking this test. Norms for interpretations are available for the age group mentioned above. Reliability and validity of all the subscales of this test are at an acceptance level. (Vroom, V.H. and Wissler, R.E. 1969)

3. **16 P.F test of R.B. Cattell:**

Raymond B. Cattell and his associates developed this 16 Personality Factors test in 1949 and the 5th edition of this test having 185 statements (items) was published in the year 1993.

The theory of Cattell emphasised two levels of behavioural traits: those which are visible, known as surface traits and the latent primary source traits derived through a rigorous statistical method called 'Factor Analysis'. He has described 46 surface traits and 16 source traits. The 16 source traits of Cattell are: (1) Warmth (2) Reasoning (3) Emotional stability (4) Dominance (5) Liveliness (6) Rule consciousness (7) Social Boldness. (8) Sensitivity (9) Vigilance. (10) Abstractedness (11) Privateness (12) Apprehension (13) openness to change (14) Self Reliance (15) Perfectionism (16) Tension.

The 16PF is built on rigorous statistical analysis and so concern for high level of reliability and validity were well addressed to. (Conn, S.R. and Rieke, M.L. 1994., Cattell, R.B. 1965; 1970 Bischof, L.J. 1970., Joe Omkim and Mueller 1978; Kroeger, O. And Thuesen, J.M. 1989)

4. **Eysenck's Personality Inventory:**

On the basis of factor analysis, Eysenck inferred three main factors: (1) Introversion Vs Extraversion. (2) Emotional instability Vs Emotional instability and (3) Psychoticism. The third factor was later deemphasised by the author. Combinations of the other two factors could result in: introverted emotional stability; Introverted emotional instability; Extroverted emotional stability; Extroverted emotional instability. Think of one vertical line as extroversion at the top and introversion at the bottom, and another horizontal line in the middle as emotional instability at the left and emotional stability at the right. The upper right part is for the extraverted emotional stability. The lower left part is introverted-emotional instability. On the top left is extroverted emotional instability and at the bottom right is introverted emotional stability. All the personality traits can be classified in any of these four segments. Interest in social affairs, leadership skills, talkativeness, lack of tension, special interest on matters in the external world etc., are seen in the upper right side, and neurotic behavioural traits at the lower left side.

There are 57 statements in the inventory and the responses to the statements are in the form of 'True/False'. A method to detect over-smart person trying to fool the test is also a part of this inventory. This test was first published in 1956. The test is also known as Eysenck's Personality questionnaire and Maudsley Personality Inventory (MPI) (Eysenck, H.J. 1998).

The reliability and validity of this test are within the acceptance limits

5. **Myers-Briggs Type Indicator (MBTI):**

Psychologist Carl Gustav Jung first wrote extensively about the two dimensions of personality i.e., Introversion and Extroversion. It was Jung who started the classification of types and other authors expanded on it by taking other dimensions.

Jung himself has expanded the types by suffixing six other descriptive categories i.e., sensing Vs intuitive introvert/extrovert; Thinking Vs. Feeling introvert/extrovert; Judging Vs Perceiving introvert/extrovert.

Cathrine C. Briggs and her daughter Isabel Briggs Myers authored MBTI based on the types of personality classified by Jung. The test consists of 100 self report items with forced choice responses. The 16 personality types developed and scored by Briggs and Myers in MBTI are as follows:

ISTJ:

Introvert/Sensing/ Thinking/Judging.

e.g. Inspector

ISFJ:

Introvert/Sensing/Feeling/Judging.

e.g. Defender

INTJ:

Introvert/Intuitive / Thinking / Judging.

e.g. Architect

INFJ:

Introvert / Intuitive / Feeling / Judging.

e.g. Advocate; Counselor

ISTP:

Introvert / Sensing / Thinking / Perceiving.

e.g. Craftsman

ISFP:

Introvert / Sensing / Feeling / Perceiving.

E.g. Adventurer

INTP:

Introvert / Intuitive / Thinking / Perceiving.

e.g. Logician/Thinker

INFP:

Introvert/ Intuitive /Feeling / Perceiving.

e.g. Mediator; Idealist

ESTJ:

Extrovert /Sensing/ Thinking/ Judging.

e.g. Executive/ supervisor

ESFJ:

Extrovert / Sensing /Feeling / Judging.

e.g. Provider

ENTJ:

Extrovert / Intuitive /Thinking /Judging.

e.g. Defender; Commander

ENFJ:

Extrovert/ Sensing/ Feeling/ Judging.

e. g. Protagonist

ESTP:

Extrovert/Sensing/Thinking/Perceiving.

e.g. Entrepreneur

ESFP:

Extrovert/sensing/Feeling/Perceiving.

e.g. Entertainer /Composer

ENTP:

Extrovert/Intuitive/Thinking/Perceiving.

e.g. Debater; Visionary

ENFP:

Extrovert/Intuitive/Feeling/ Perceiving.

e.g. Campaigner

Critics of MBTI say that the test is a pseudoscientific self report questionnaire without any clarity on reliability and validity of the test. (Kroeger, O and Thuesen, J.M. 1989., Jung, C.G. 1921)

6. **The DiSC (Dominance, influence, Steadiness, Compliance):**

This test was developed by William Mouton Marston Psychologist with a Harvard Ph.D. The term 'Dominance' reflects behaviour characteristics of assertive result oriented social leader. The 'influence' (Please note that it is 'i' and not 'I' in capital letter as a trade mark held by M/s. John Wiley and Sons) reflects characteristics associated with effective and cordial interpersonal relations. The letter 'S' stands for steadiness reflecting behavioural qualities such as patience, cooperation, effective team work etc. And the final 'C' stands for conscientiousness/ compliance reflecting precision and quality of work performance, attention to details, systematic methodical etc.

Application of DiSC is made popular in business and industry by the consultancy M/s Thomas International Personality Profile Analysis.

The DiSC test consists of 80 questions and it takes approximately 20 minutes to complete the test performance. (Scullard, M and Baum, B. 2015., Barens, L.V. and Narde, D. 2014)

7. **The Big Five Factor Model Personality Test:**

This is a popular test approved by academic psychologists because of its scientific base. The five factors mentioned in the test are as follows:

(1) Openness (2) Conscientiousness (3) Extroversion (4) Agreeableness (5) Neuroticism. This test is also known as OCEAN, an abbreviation of all the five factors.

The trait 'Openness' is the quality of being curious and readiness to experiment with new ways of doing. Fear, anxiety and conservative mind set is the other extreme of 'openness'.

'Conscientiousness' refers to the behavioural quality of being sincere and honest commitment to a purpose in life. The opposite of this factor is indifference to performance and related matters.

'Extroversion' reflects the behaviour quality of being outgoing in social relations and enthusiastic on external matters. The opposite is 'Introversion', the quality of being socially withdrawn and lethargic.

'Agreeableness' refers to warm and cordial relationship with others at one extreme and the opposite of cold and unpleasant interpersonal relationship on the other side.

'Neuroticism' is a trait that reflects either emotional stability on the positive side or emotional instability as the negative opposite. Woks of R. B. Cattell and his collaborators and further advancement by others were subjected to further factor analysis by Digman, J.M., Lewis Goldman, Costa and McCrae and others. The speciality of this test is the condensation of all possible traits into a meaningful five factors.

The reliability and validity indices of this test are above 0.70 which is considered as acceptable. (McCrae, R.R and Juri Allik, 2002., Wiggins, 1996;

8. **Hogan Personality Inventory (HPI):**

The purpose of the Hogan Personality Inventory is to find out what a person's positive aspects are in his/her relationships with others and also in demonstrating their own abilities. Created in the 1980s, this test is based on the Big Five Factor Model and focuses on social relationships. The test consists of seven basic scales, six vocational scales and 42 other subscales. Adjustment, Ambition, Sociability, Interpersonal Sensitivity, Prudence, Inquisitiveness and Learning Approach are the seven basic dimensions mentioned in this test. This test can be completed in fifteen to twenty minutes.

The reliability and validity indices of this test are within the acceptable range. (Hogen, R et. al., 2007):

Glossary of Terms:

Achievement tests: When the purpose of the test is assessment of the benefits attained as a consequence of training/teaching, it is called an achievement test.

Aptitude tests: Assessment of potential abilities for Certain job or future studies

Behavioural dispositions: The tendency to behave; not the actual behaviour, but a prediction of the possible actual behaviour.

Behavioural traits: Behavioural dispositions on certain qualities

Cardinal traits: Dominant traits that influence our behaviour

Common traits: A trait that is found in all individuals with varying proportion.

Concept validity: A measure of the attainment of the Purpose, i.e., whether the test measures what it intended to measure.

Concurrent validity: When a test scores agree with the scores obtained in another well established test measuring the same attribute, the measure of agreement between the two tests is an indication of the concurrent validity.

Connotation: The qualitative meaning of a term.

Construct validity: A construct is the concept (the psychological attribute) which cannot be directly observed, but is inferred from observable behavioural symptoms. Intelligence is a construct, a concept inferred by certain exhibited actions of the person.

Cronbach Alpha: A statistical measure of internal consistency.

Denotation: The quantitative distribution of a term.

Difficulty level: Percentage of respondents who have answered the correct alternative or the desirable alternative; Low percentage indicates high difficulty level and high percentage is an indication of easy items.

Discrimination value/index: A value/index that differentiates the response of the high scoring group from the low scoring group.

Factor Analysis: A statistical method to infer the existence of a latent factor among various attributes, based on correlations.

Group discussion: A situational test to assess specific behavioural characteristics in a group, such as, leadership initiative, participation on the theme of discussion, communication skills, encouragement, support to other participating members etc.

Group test: When a test is administered to a large number of individuals at one place at the same time, it is termed as group test.

Individual test: When a test is administered to a single individual, it is termed as individual test.

Interval scale: When the distances between the adjacent numbers are equal, it is termed as an interval scale. No multiplication/ division is possible without an absolute zero (nonexistence of the attribute) at the bottom of the measurement.

Item analysis: The statistical method of finding the difficulty level and the discrimination values of the sample items so that only items having high discrimination values are selected for the final test items.

Measurement: Quantification of any attribute and method of assessing its amount is a measurement.

Neuroticism: Emotional instability such as fear, anxiety worry, obsessive thought/feeling/ and/or compulsive action etc. The person under neuroticism is otherwise normal without losing the time and space orientations.

Nominal scale: When the measurement is for identification of the attribute with a number or descriptive label, it is a nominal scale. 1,2,3 ...n or male Vs female, child, adult, old age etc are nominal scales.

Operational definition: Assessment of an inferred quality of behaviour by observation and measurement of observed behavioural symptoms.

Ordinal scale: When the quantity measured is in terms of greater than or less than marking such measurements in the form of rank order, it is called an ordinal scale.

Paper-Pencil tests: When the responses of the person being tested is on a piece of paper, then it is called a paper-pencil test.

Percentile: A measure of the level of the scores in terms of percentage of people below a certain stage. If a person is at the 80th percentile, it means that 79 percentage of people who have taken the test are below his/her level.

Performance tests: Actual activity associated with the attribute being measured. Finger dexterity test, eye-hand coordination test, driving test etc. are examples.

Personal Interview: A situational test to assess the suitability of the person to a position or to collect the personal views of a known person on certain issues.

Predictive validity: Checking whether the prediction made by the observation of test scores is supported by certain exhibited behaviour is the predictive validity. i.e., matching the examination scores with the prediction of high intelligence.

Projective tests: Analysis of the responses of a person to a semi-structured or unstructured situation such as Rorchach Inkblot test, Sentence completion test, draw a man test, Thematic Apperception test etc. and its interpretations on the assumption that such responses are the projected thoughts and feeling of the person responding to such stimuli.

Psychological attribute: Behavioural characteristics/ mental qualities being measured.

Psychological test: Any test, with or without quantification relating to mind/behaviour is a psychological test.

Psychometric test: When a test is based on quantification for measurement and standardized for interpretation, it becomes a psychometric test.

Psychoticism: insanity i.e. loss of time and space orientation in one's behaviour/mind set.

Ratio scale: An interval scale with an absolute zero at the bottom of the measurement so that multiplication and division are possible.

Reliability: The self consistency of the items in the test Cronbach's Alpha) and also response consistency of the test takers when the tests are taken at different times (test retest method) or high positive correlation between responses (consistency) to even and odd items of the test (Split half method) or consistency of responses in two equivalent tests (Equivalent form method)

sample items: Reflections of behavioural traits in the form of certain statements with structured responses for endorsement or rejection.

Scales: A measurement tool is a scale. Selection of sample items: Reducing the number of collected sample items by the statistical treatment of item analysis of the responses received by a sample respondents.

Situational tests: observation of behaviour/performance by a group of experts and assessment on a rating scale. Interview performance, group discussion etc. are examples

Source traits: The latent common factor among several traits.

Standardization: The statistical method of observing the frequency distribution of test scores and then interpreting the test scores either in the form of percentile in the case of non-normal distribution or in the form of standard distribution scores known as z score or its percentile values.

Standard Deviation: The deviation score from the mean in a normal distribution. The standard score of the mean is considered as zero.

Surface traits: Observed behavioural traits associated with a latent common factor.

Test- rest reliability: (see reliability)

Validity: A statistical index on what it measures. If it measures what it intended to measure, then its validity is very high.

References:

Aiken, L.R. (2012)

Psychological Testing and Assessment.

London: Pearson.

Allen. J.M. (2004).,

Introduction to Measurement Theories.

Illinois: Waveland Press, Inc.

Allport, G.W. (1961).,

Pattern and Growth in Personality

New York: Holt, Rinehart and Winston

Allport, G.W. (1937).,

Personality: A Psychological Interpretation.

New York: Holt, Rinehart and Winston.

Barens, L.V and Narde, Daria. (2004).,

Understanding Yourself and Others: An Introduction to Personality Type Code.

New York: Telos Publications.

Bischof L.J. (1970).,

Interpreting Personality Theories.

New York: Harper & Row.

Carter Philip. (2008).,

Psychometric Testing: 1000 Ways to Assess Your Personality, Creativity, Intelligence and Lateral Thinking.

London: Kogan Page.

Cattell, R.B. (1970).,

Handbook for the 16PF Questionnare.

Illinois: IPAT (Institute for Personality and Ability Testing)

Cattell, R.B. (1965).,

The Scientific Analysis of Personality

London: Penguin Books.

Cohen R.J. Swerdlik, M.E. (2017).,

Psychological Testing and Assessment: An Introduction to Tests and Measurement.

New York: McGrow Hill Education.

Conn, S.R. and Rieke, M.L. (1994).,

The 16PF Fifth Edition Technical Manual.

Illinois: IPAT.

DeVellis, R.F. (2016).,

Measurement Scales in Research: Methodological Perspectives.

New York: Guildford Press.

Eysenck, H.J. (1998).,

Dimensions of Personality

New Jersey: Transaction Publishers.

Furr, R.M. and Bacharach V.R. (2013).,

Psychometrics: An Introduction.

California: SAGE Publications.

Gregory, R.J. (2013).,

Psychological Testing: History, Principles and Applications.

London: Pearson.

Hogan, Robert; Hogan Joyce, and Warrenfelts, R.B. (2007).,

The Hogan Guide: Interpretation and Use of Hogan Inventories.

Oklahoma: Hogan Assessment Systems, Inc.

Jae-Omkin and Mueller, C.W. (1978).,

Factor Analysis: Statistical Methods and Practical Issues.

New York: SAGE Publications.

James R.M, et. al. (2018).,

Measurement and Evaluation of Human Performance.

(Publisher): Human Kinetics.

Jung, C.G. (1923).,

Psychological Types

New York: Harcourt Brace and Company

Kaplan, David et. al. (2004).,

The SAGE Handbook of Quantitative Methodology for Social Sciences.

California: SAGE publications.

Kohn, A.A. (2017).,

Development of Psychological Assessment and Testing.

New York: Springer.

Kroeger, Otto and Thuesen, J.M. (1989).,

Type Talk: The 16 Personality Types that Determine How We Live, Love and Work.

New York: Dell.

Marston, W.M. (1979).,

Emotions of Normal People.

San Francisco: Persona Press.

McCrae, R.R. and Juri Allik. (2002).,

The BIG Five Personality Traits: The Five Factor Model of Personality Across Cultures.

New York: Springer.

Oliver P. John., Richard, W.R. and: Lawrence, A.P. (2008).,

Handbook of Personality: Theory and Research
New York: The Guildford Press.

Price, L.R. (2017).,

Psychometrics: Theory into Practice.

New York: Guildford Press.

Scullard, Mark and Baum, Dabney. (2015).,

Everything DiSC Manual.

New Jersey: John Wiley and Sons.

Urbina Susana. (2014).,

Essentials of Psychological Testing.

New Jersey: John Wiley.

Vroom, V.H. (1969).,

The California Psychological Inventory Handbook

California: Consulting Psychologists Press.

Wiggins, J.S. (1996).,

The Five Factor Model of Personality.

New York: Guilford Press.

Chapter 5

Construction of a psychometric test for the assessment of a happy, successful person

The Background of the study:

As a member of the Faculty, teaching and consulting in the area of Organizational behaviour and human resource management in the school of Management Studies, Cochin University of Science and Technology, my prime area of interest was the personal attributes required for a happy, successful, effective and efficient manager. Review of available literature, and personal discussion with a large number of practising managers have come to the conclusion to the following attributes or personal qualities: decision making ability without procrastination; self control over one's own actions; skills in interpersonal and social relations; leadership capability; positive attitude towards self and others; effective communication and negotiation skills, expertise in certain knowledge domain; Cognitive competence; emotional intelligence; attention to details and tolerance to diversities. Further studies have revealed that there is no single test available in the field to measure all these qualities, and also capable of administrating within an hour and without taxing too much on the person being assessed?

We need a multiphase inventory with several subscales to assess several personal qualities mentioned above in one test. By multiphase, we mean a single test material that measures several qualities at the same time. Analysis of various test inventories available on the subject revealed that test items (statements) as a whole does not measure any specific attribute, but a cluster of items known as sub scales do measure specific personal attributes. One such available Inventory is the Minnesota Multiphasic Personality Inventory -- MMPI. This instrument consists of 566 statements with ten subscales as clinical instruments to classify and categorise unhealthy mental conditions. The ten subscales are: (1.) Hypochondriasis (Hs): i.e. a person's preoccupation with his/her health and body functions (2) Depression (D): i.e. mood at inactive low level (3) Hysteria (Hy): i.e. general level of emotionality with physical body symptoms of inner mental disorders. (4) Psychopathic Deviate: i.e. amorality and undesirable social deviations considered as crime (5) Masculinity-Femininity (Mf): i.e. the traditional gender roles and interests in a given society (6) Paranoia (Pa): i.e. suspicious and lack of trust and other unrealistic thoughts and emotions (7) Psychasthenia (Pt): i.e. anxiety, unrealistic fears and obsessive and compulsive behaviour (8) Schizophrenia (Sc): i.e. social alienation, and unrealistic perceptions and thoughts (9) Hypomania (Ha): i.e. elevated mood, energy and irritability (10) Social Introversion (Si): shy and socially withdrawn type. These ten categories for diagnostic purpose are the selected items per subscales from the 566 items and nothing is measured by using all the 566 items together. The 566 statements are like a dictionary of statements on all possible mental health and illness. The given statements are to be approved or rejected by the respondents by saying 'True' or 'False'. Most of the personality inventories now available are statements borrowed from the MMPI.

The author of this book happened to get a copy of the entire statements of MMPI from a psychology department and thought of reducing the items for the use of matured normal human adults – college educated of 20 years Plus age both male and female—Indian respondents. (Respondents limited to Kerala of India). MMPI is not a culture free test and hence the need for standardizing the test for the Indian subjects was felt by the author. A reduced number of 92 items from 566 items is the result of empirical research on the endorsement of statements by 150 practising managers who were part time students in the school of Management Studies. It was not possible to administer the entire test of 566 items at one sitting. The test was, therefore, divided into five sections of 120 statements in four sections and 86 items in the last 5th section. The statements were taken in transparency sheets for projection on the board. The 120 statements took 40 to 60 minutes for responding. The test was not a time-bound test nor a difficulty bound. Instruction was to respond in the form of TRUE or FALSE with comments on items which were not easy to comprehend. At one stage the reduction was up to 128 and later with the introduction of fulltime MBA for youngsters above 19 years of age, but below 26 years, more respondents were taken for the empirical study of endorsement to the statements. The final reduction statement at this final stage became 92. The method of arriving at 92 statements was as follows: (1) where more than 75% of the respondents endorsed an item (marked as 'True' or 'False', it represents commonality and hence the item does not differentiate the respondents. Rejection of items based on this criterion was 97. (2) If the endorsement of an item was less than 26%, then it was a minority among the respondents indicating the possibility of deviant responses more applicable to the mentally ill people. Rejection of items by this criterion was 201. Thus items more relevant to normal human adults were selected by using these criteria for rejection. (3) Another criterion for rejection was Directional deviations in the endorsements for which a comparison with the endorsement of American normal adult subjects was required. Data on the American normal college educated adults was available in the 'An MMPI Handbook' of Dahlstrom and Welsh (Dahlstrom, W.G and Welsh, G.S., 1960 pp 417-429). When 60% of American subjects endorsed a statement as 'True' but only 20% Indians endorse it or vice-versa, then it is an indication of directional deviation. Such directional deviations show the cultural impact. Moreover, the scoring will also be affected by such directional deviations. The items thus rejected by this criterion of directional deviation were 85. (4) One among the repeated pair items (not rejected by other criteria) was also excluded. Such rejection came to 03. (There were a total of 16 pairs (32 in total) repeat items of which 29 items were already rejected by other criteria). (5) Statements with reference to a particular book or a particular religion or any such specific reference items were also removed. Statements that created problems of easy comprehension such as difficult words, American slangs and phrases, double negative expressions etc were also rejected by the criterion of language /culture/ specific reference etc. Items thus rejected by this criterion came to 88. These rejections by 5 criteria were based on the endorsement of items by the Indian subjects. There could be some items rejected by the American subjects, but acceptable to the Indian subjects. Rejection by Indians but, acceptable by the Americans is also possible.

The total rejected items were 474 leaving behind 92 (474+92=566) as the short form of MMPI for the use of normal human adults (college educated above 19 years of age both male and female).

All the 92 statements are not used as a single test for assessment. Only subscale items prepared by several researchers are used.

There are 213 such subscales given in the MMPI Handbook by Dahlstrom and Welsh (1960, pp 448-468). The author selected only those subscales which were found relevant to the selection of managerial personnel. The subscales thus selected are: (1) Dependency (Navran, 1954); Original MMPI (OM) items: 57 Short MMPI (SM) items: 15 items). (2) Hostility (Cook and Medley, 1954—OM: 50; SM: 20. (3) Emotional Immaturity (Pearson, 1954; OM: 48; SM: 11). (4) Emotional Impulsivity (Gough, 1957; OM: 21; SM: 8. (5) Social Introversion (Welsh, 1952; OM: 50; SM: 13. (6) Leadership (Gough, 1957; OM: 50; SM: 15. (7) Attitude towards Self (Gibson, 1955; OM: 20; SM: 8. (8) Attitude towards Others (Gibson, 1955; OM: 20; SM: 7. (9) Teaching potentiality (Gowan and Gowan, 1955; OM: 98; SM: 13. (10) Counsellor personality (Cottle, Lewin and Penney, 1954; OM: 51, SM: 12(11) K-Scale (Mckenley, Hathway and Meehl, 1948; OM: 30; SM: 11. (12) L-Scale (Hathway and McKenley 1951; OM: 15; SM: 6. The last two scales mentioned above are for the purpose of exclusion of the respondent who is deliberately creating a positive impression by giving the best possible answers and not his/her actual feelings and thoughts. These two subscales, in fact, are reliability scales for identifying persons whose responses are not reliable.

Most of the subscales mentioned above are measuring mental ill health or negative traits. To make it positive, the inverse score was used with inverse positive traits. The term 'Dependency' was changed into

'Psychological Autonomy'; 'Hostility' into 'Intimacy'; 'Immaturity' into 'Decisiveness'; 'Impulsivity' into 'Self Control'; 'Social Introversion' into 'Social Extroversion'. Other traits such a 'Leadership', 'Attitude towards Self' ('Self Esteem'), 'Attitude towards Others' ('Regard for others'), 'Teaching Potentiality' and 'Counsellor Personality' were retained as they are positive expressions of the traits.

The study report is now based on a 92 item short MMPI with 12 subscales (10+2 subscales). Personality traits assessed by the subscales are: (1) Psychological Autonomy, (2) Intimacy, (3) Decisiveness, (4) Self Control, (5) Social Extroversion, (6) Leadership, (7) Self Esteem, (8) Regard for Others (9) Teaching Potentiality with focus on communication skill and (10) Counsellor personality with focus on empathetic understanding. The additional 2 subscales, K-scale (McKinsey and Hathaway, 1948) and L-scale (Hathaway S.R. and Mckinsey, J.C. 1951) are on response reliability for acceptance or rejection of the responses given by the person.

All the 92 statements are not relevant to the selected 10+2 subscales. There are many items not useful for the measurement of specified traits; but they are retained as the test items are an abridgements of MMPI for the use of other traits not selected by the author. Some of the items are common for many subscales.

It may be noted that another criterion was also used for rejection of certain items with specific reference to the selected subscales. This criterion was 'Discrimination value/discrimination index of the item. As such a criterion was with specific reference to the subscales, rejection of such items with less discrimination values was confined to the subscales and not for the shortened form of MMPI with 92 items.

The method of finding the discrimination index is as follows: Arrange the scores obtained by the respondents in an ascending order and create two groups i.e., A high group with high scores and a low group who scored low. Find out the number of people with correct responses in both groups and adopt the formula high + Low divided by total N/2. The discrimination index may vary from 0.0 to 1.0. Test items with less than 0.3 discrimination indices were rejected.

The statistical analysis for finding differences due to age, gender, academic faculty background, standardization for classifications and interpretations, reliability, validity etc are discussed in detail in the concerned chapters from 6 to 10. However, observations on the common features of all the specific subscales are to be highlighted here in this chapter. Correlations among the 10 traits are relevant in asking the question whether these 10 traits can be reduced further to a lower number, based on factor analysis method; this was carried out and the finding was that there were only two factors. One of the factors is socio-emotive factor or people orientation factor and the other is cognitive emotive factor or performance orientation factor. Psychological autonomy, intimacy, social extroversion, leadership, self esteem, regards for others, teaching potentiality and counsellor personality are the traits that belong to the latent factor 'People Orientation' as the loading of these traits are above 0. 70. The other latent factor of 'Performance Orientation' with moderate loading values of 0. 50 to 0.60 consist of two traits of decisiveness and self control. Chapter 11 dealing with combination of these two latent factors is labelled as 'personal Efficacy' i.e., effective and efficient task performance with cordial and pleasant emotive behaviour. This test constructed by the author need some label and so I have given a name for the test: Poduval's Personal Efficacy Test (PPET).

Chapters 6 to 11 are dealing with the personality traits associated with effective and efficient manager or with Happy and successful persons in general. Chapter 12 is devoted to the discussion of other factors related to happiness with success and also training programmes available for improvement of deficiencies in personal efficacy.

Glossary of Terms:

Attention to details: Perceiving all the details in a particular situation or environment by concentration.

Attitude towards others: High or low positive attitude towards others or simply high or low regard for other people.

Attitude towards self: High or low positive attitude toward self or simply Self esteem.

Autonomy vs. Independence: Freedom to take one's own decision and action without any desire for appreciation and approval of other people is autonomy whereas freedom from others is independence.

Cognitive competence: Ability in perceiving and thinking in task performance, problem solving and decision making

Communication: Common understanding between a speaker and his/her listener or between the transmitter and the receiver.

Counsellor personality: A person who helps others by his/her empathic understanding of the problems of his/her clients.

Culture free test: A test wherein the impact of tradition and culture (group differences) is eliminated.

Decisiveness: Ability to take prompt decisions i.e., the time taken for taking a decision is optimal or short.

Dependency: The disposition/ mind set of seeking help, support and appreciation from others in decision making and actions.

Depression: A mental condition of low level of activity with an unhappy mood.

Directional deviation: A majority-minority inverse relationship between two groups of people. If one group is maintaining a high positive attitude towards a particular issue and the other group is exhibiting low positive attitude, then they are in opposite camp or in directional deviation.

Effective: A condition of attaining a set goal or accomplishing a set task.

Efficient: A condition of maintaining economy in time, effort and utilization of resources.

Emotional intelligence: All non-cognitive personality factors including feelings and emotions that affect task performance, problem solving and decision making processes.

Empathy: The mindset to feel the feelings of others with whom a person is interacting.

Femininity: certain women - like behavioural and cultural qualities.

Happy: A mental condition of positive well-being. It consists of positive emotions, engagement, positive relationship with others, motivation or high energy and a sense of achievement (PERMA of Seligmann).

Hostility: Negative feelings and assumptions with respect to others. Low level of hostility is taken as intimacy.

Hypochondrias: irrational anxiety and fear of physical illness in spite of reassurance of healthy conditions by medical practitioners.

Hypomania: High level of activity with a pleasant mood, but not as severe as seen in bipolar illness.

Hysteria: An emotional and behavioural condition of split personality with anxiety, fear, fainting etc which cannot be explained by the normal functioning of the body.

Immaturity: A not fully developed condition in the growth process i.e., low maturity level in the growth process resulting in wavering and indecisions

Impulsivity: An immediate action without much thinking on the consequences of certain decisions. The opposite of impulsivity is self control.

Interpersonal relations: Relationship between two interacting persons.

Intimacy: The readiness to share one's views and experiences with another person without any reservation and inhibition and also readiness to sacrifice one's time and resources for the benefit of the other.

Leadership: The role of taking responsibility of directing and controlling a group of people

Manager: One who takes the role of directing and controlling certain number of subordinates for the attainment of goals set by the employing organization.

Masculinity: Certain behavioural characteristics that are typical of the male gender

MMPI: Minnesota Multiphasic Personality Inventory consists of 566 items/statements with several subscales for the measurement of innumerable personality traits, especially traits associated with mental illness.

Multiphasic: An inventory of test items with several subscales for the measurement of many specific personality traits; A test inclusive of all items of inventory need not be there in a multiphasic test.

Negotiation: interpersonal or intergroup communication for arriving at a common understanding on certain issues.

Paranoia: False belief that others are after the person to harm him/her. Sometimes it could even be a false belief or delusion of grandeur or self greatness, instead of false belief of persecution.

Procrastination: The tendency to take too much time for taking a decision and implementing the same.

Psychesthania: An outdated expression for the behaviour pattern associated with irrational fear, obsessions with some ideas, compulsive actions, excessive anxiety etc.

Psychopathic deviate: Socially deviant with a tendency to involve in criminal activities.

Regard for others: Positive attitude towards other people with whom one is interacting.

Schizophrenia: A type of mental illness with the symptom of withdrawal from social life, brooding over some thoughts on oneself with a depressive mood.

Self control: The disposition or mindset t to control impulsive actions

Self esteem: Positive attitude towards self or the tendency to perceive all good things about self.

Social extroversion: A behavioural disposition to be actively involved in group and social activities; an outgoing personality.

Social introversion: A behavioural disposition to withdraw from social relations; opposite to an outgoing personality; social alienation and isolation are the behavioural symptoms of a social introvert.

Successful: The condition of being accomplished the set goals by an individual with or without happiness.

Teaching potentiality: The potential personal dispositions and behavioural skills of an effective and efficient communication of an effective teacher.

Tolerance to diversities: A receptive orientation of a person to view and review cultural differences without any value judgements.

References:

Cook, W.W and Medley, D.M. (1954).,

"Proposed hostility and pharisaic-virtue scale for the MMPI".

J. Appl. Psychology, 1954, 38, 414-418.

Cottle, W.C., and Lewin, W.W. (1954).,

"Personal characteristics of counsellors: II. Male counsellor responses to the MMPI CZTS".

J. Counsel. Psychology, 1954, 1, 27-30.

Cottle, W.C., and Penney M.M. (1954).,

"Personal characteristics of counsellors:III. An Experimental Scale".

J. Counsel. Psychology, 1954, 1, 74-77.

Dahlstrom, W.G and Welsh, G.S. (1960).,

An MMPI Handbook: A Guide to use in clinical practice and research.

Minneapolis: The University of Minnesota Press

Gibson, R.L. (1955).,

A Factor Analysis of Measures of Change Following Client Centred Therapy.

PhD. Dissertation, Pennsylvania State University.

Gough, H.C. (1957).,

California Psychological Inventory Manual.

Palo Alto: Consulting Psychologists Press.

Gowan, J.C. and Gowan, Mary, S. (1955).,

"A teacher prognosis scale for the MMPI"

J. Educ. Research, 1955, 49, 1-12.

Hathaway, S.R. and McKinley, J.C. (1951).,

The Minnesota Multiphasic Personality Inventory Manual (Revised)

New York: The Psychological Corporation.

McKinley, J.C., Hathaway, S.R. and, Meehl, P.E., (1948).,

"The MMPI:VI. The K scale".

J. Consult. Psychology, 1948, 12, 20-31.

Navran, L. (1954).,

"A rationally derived MMPI scale to measure dependence".

J. Consult. Psychology, 1954, 18, 192.

Pearson, J.S. (1954).,

Psychometric correlates of emotional immaturity.

Ph.D dissertation, University of Minnesota.

Welsh, G.S. (1952).,

"A factor study of the MMPI using scales with items overlapping eliminated"

American Psychologist, 1952, 7, 341.

Chapter 6

Assertive behaviour

How to attain happiness with success in your personal life and sustained effectiveness and efficiency in your professional life?

Step 1: Be Assertive in your interpersonal relations

The nature of assertive behaviour will be discussed after explaining two important components/traits of assertiveness. The behaviour patterns of assertiveness, dominance, submissiveness and aggressiveness are the products of certain combination of psychological autonomy and intimacy traits.

Psychological Autonomy/Dependency:

This trait is the inverse of psychological dependency. There is a subscale of Dependency in MMPI developed by Navran (Navran, 1954). Here, the term 'dependency' is defined as a psychological need for recognition, acceptance, and appreciation by the significant others. (Ryan, R.M. & Deci, E.L. 2017; Grey, John, 2005) Social dependency and financial dependency are different aspects of psychological dependency. The inverse of psychological dependency is psychological autonomy implying that a high score in dependency is interpreted as low autonomy and a high level of autonomy is interpreted as low dependency. Special features of the sub scale of dependency are: (1) In the dependency scale developed by Navran, (Navran, L. 1954) there were 57 items and this was reduced to 18 by the application of five criteria mentioned earlier. This 18 was further reduced to 15 by the application of discrimination index.

1. Distribution of the scores among 500 respondents is normal and so the interpretation could be by the percentile of the z- scores.

2. There is no significant difference between male and female respondents

3. There is no significant difference among the age group 20-25 years, but the age group beyond 25 years is significantly more autonomous than the younger age groups. However, as the difference in the norm for interpretation was only marginal, the same norm is used for all age groups.

4. There are no significant differences among the respondents of different academic Faculty such as BA/BSc/B.Com/B.B.A./B.C.A etc.

5. Correlations of autonomy with social extroversion, leadership, and teaching potentiality are high above 0.70 levels; correlations with self esteem and counsellor personality are moderate of being 0.50 to 0.70.

6. Reliability value of the test is above 0.80 levels and the validity value is above 0.90. Reliability was worked out by split half method and validity by self rating with the test results.

Some research findings on the Psychological Autonomy/Dependency:

The exact opposite word of psychological dependency is independence and why the word psychological autonomy is used in place of independence? Independent implies freedom from others, where as autonomy means freedom to take one's own decision and actions without a need to get approval, appreciation, and recognition from others. Dependence could be social dependence as in the case of a child clinging on the parents or financial dependency on others for survival and development. Psychological dependency implies a mental condition of becoming a shadow to someone else or clinging on others for approval, appreciation etc. Similarly autonomy could mean institutional freedom from some other agency, wherein decentralization of authority is at the focus. Psychological autonomy implies individual autonomy or freedom to take one's own decisions and action, thus making it a self responsibility by maintaining individuality. It implies self sufficiency and capability to take informed, but unenforced decisions. (Ryan and Deci, 2017). In such situations, one does not bother about what others may think of such decisions and actions.

Some significant research findings are: Higher levels of autonomy is associated with better mental health; Greater level of autonomy implies lower level of depression and anxiety and higher levels of self esteem and life satisfaction; higher level of autonomy fosters intrinsic motivation for better task performance, problem solving and decision making; Authoritarian or permissive paternal style may lead to poor autonomy in the child. The authoritarian style implies strong control and weak warmth, while permissive style fosters lower level of control and higher level of warmth; high resilience of quick readjustment to unexpected misfortunes in life is more pronounced among the psychological autonomous group of people; the culture including gender role differences of a community is also a significant factor that influences the level of psychological autonomy (Grey, John. 2005).

Hostility/Intimacy:

Another component of assertive behaviour pattern is intimacy, the inverse of hostility developed by Cook and Medley (1954). In the scale developed by Cook and Medley on hostility, there were 50 items which were reduced to 23 and a further reduction to 20 items by the application of discrimination index. Intimacy, the inverse of hostility is defined as the readiness of the person to share his/her experiences without any reservation and inhibition and also ready to sacrifice time and resources for the benefit of the other person with whom he/she is intimate. Hostility is the negative side of intimacy implying that high hostility is low intimacy and low hostility is high intimacy. Score distribution is normal for the applications of parametric statistics. The norm prepared was in the form of percentile of z-scores. There are no significant differences of age, gender and academic faculty and so the norm for interpretation is common to all. Correlations of intimacy with other traits are as follows: Strong correlations: Teaching potentiality and counsellor personality; Moderate correlation with: leadership, self esteem and regard for others. Reliability of the scale is acceptable as the correlation index is above 0.70. Validity index is also high.

Some research findings on intimacy/hostility:

There are different types of intimacy – emotional intimacy, physical intimacy, intellectual intimacy, experiential intimacy etc.

The common feature among all these different forms of intimacy is reduced physical and mental distance between two individuals, mutual sharing of information and experiences, and readiness to sacrifice time and resources for the benefit of the other.

Some of the research findings on intimacy are: Trust, mutual understanding and empathy are essential for romantic intimacy; sharing of experiences and information by self disclosers is required for the development of emotional intimacy; intimacy between two individual may be hindered by anxiety oriented attachments; be free with your body for better intimacy, especially with romantic intimacy; sharing of knowledge and information is the essential aspect of intellectual intimacy; a feeling of togetherness is an integral part of experiential intimacy; modern information technology and other forms of technological mechanisms are likely to reduce the level of intimacy; Conditioning and control of intimacy is possible by the nature of culture of a community.

The combination effect:

When we combine psychological autonomy and intimacy, it may result in four possible behaviour patterns in interpersonal relations. The possible behaviour patterns by the combination are: (1) assertiveness

(2) Dominance (3) Submissiveness and (4) Aggressiveness. The picture given below shows the effect of combination:

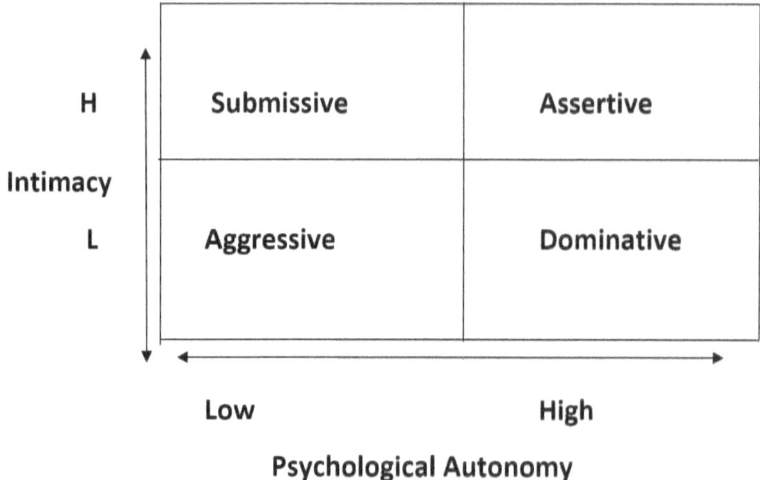

As seen in the above picture, a high-high combination of psychological autonomy and intimacy results in assertive type of behaviour; a high-low combination results in dominative type; a low-high level effect is submissiveness and a low-low combination results in aggressive type.

Research findings on the four behaviour patterns in interpersonal relations:

Assertive:

It is a behavioural-social skill associated with cordial and pleasant relationship with others and honest communication without hurting the feeling of others. It is to be differentiated from dominance by the presence or absence of intimacy; high intimacy in assertiveness and low intimacy in dominance, though high autonomy is common to both. Assertiveness is positively associated with leadership initiative, social extroversion and self esteem, personal well-being and mental health. It is also associated with professional competency and life satisfaction. It is possible to enhance the level of assertiveness by role modelling method of training.

Assertiveness is positively correlated with self empowerment, internal locus of control, self esteem and self confidence, job satisfaction, extroversion and leadership and professional advancement.

(Paterson, R.J. 2022; Malandro, L. 2014; Murphy, J. 2011).

Dominative:

A high level autonomy with low level intimacy results in the dominative style of behaviour in interpersonal relations. Autonomy is common to both assertiveness and dominance, but in intimacy they differ: high intimacy in assertiveness and low intimacy in dominance. This distinction is not often mentioned in most literature on the assumption that both are synonyms. Look at the dictionary for their meanings. Assertiveness is defined as dominance and dominance is defined as assertiveness. Dominant people may produce the expected results in the short run, but not in the long run as their followers may resent the lack of intimacy in the dealings of their leader and sometimes may deliberately work against the interest of their leader. Under crisis situations people may forget absence of intimacy and work together with the dominant leader, but the same condition may not be there under peaceful situations. The essential difference between authoritarian and democratic regimes is this difference between dominant and assertive leadership styles.

A dominating person is decisive, competitive, and proactive with high self esteem and confidence. However, the person will experience stress and conflict with others in interpersonal relations. He/she strives to take up leadership roles, but their influence on the team members will be at a lower level unless the person is very competent in his/her profession. In most communities men are dominant, but there are some communities where women are more dominant than men. It all depends on economic status and education of men and women. Stress and burnout are the two negative consequences of extreme dominative behaviour. (Ringer, R. 1984; Potter, D. 2020; Fromm, E. 2013; Konrad, L 1974)

Submissive:

When the intimacy is high, but autonomy is low, the combination effect is submissiveness. The submissive people are apparently very calm and quiet always following the directions of the boss, but eventually may turn to be aggressive. A person who is submissive to the boss but dominative to his/her subordinates is basically an aggressive person showing two different behaviour styles to suite the purpose. Even among the husband-wife partnership, this kind of submissive person turning to aggressive is common. However the reverse of aggressive person becoming submissive never happens, though they may become assertive.

Submissive people generally yield to the wishes of others for maintaining harmony and for avoiding conflicts. They experience high anxiety at disharmony and lower self esteem. Social compliance is their general behaviour pattern. Submissive people often suppress their ill feelings and so they are likely to experience anxiety and depression. Dissatisfaction and unexpressed resentments experienced by the submissive type people may result in making them aggressive in the long run. Most submissive people are less effective in their communication. (Fromm, Erich. 1994; 2022).

Aggressive:

Low level of autonomy and low level of intimacy results in an aggressive style. The essential feature of aggression is hurting the feelings of the other by words or actions. There is some silent aggressive behaviour such as being indifferent to instructions by the higher ups, though other symptoms are lacking (Potter, D. 2020; Konrad, L. 1974' Fromm. E. 2913).

The model recommended for happiness with success is assertive behaviour style in interpersonal relations. All other styles are dysfunctional in the long run, though apparently ok in the short run. Assertive behaviour is positively associated with mental health and well being.

Negative attitude and feeling of hostility are the two aspects of aggressiveness. Tendency to attack or hurt the feelings of others are the outcome. They try to dominate over others, but often fail in their wish to be prominent. They tend to become neurotic, impulsive with a feeling of inferiority. Low self esteem and feeling of inadequacy are also seen in such people. Impairment of effective communication is also associated with aggressive behaviour. There are two types of aggressiveness:

1. Proactive aggression with focus on tendency to dominate.

2. Reactive aggression with a tendency to express anger and other negative emotions. It is possible to reduce aggressiveness by certain training programmes such as anger management, cognitive behaviour therapy, mindfulness, relaxation exercises etc.

(From, Eric. 2013; Potter, D. 2020).

Glossary of Terms:

Aggressive: Words and actions that hurt the feelings of others.

Assertive: An active person who takes decision and action at his/her own will without bothering what others may think of him/her and this kind of behaviour is by respecting the freedom of the other to be their own self.

Diffident: One who is meek, timid and unassuming with anxiety and fear in facing new situations in life.

Dominative: Desire or action to control others to become oneself more prominent and significant.

Emotional intimacy: Emotional attachment between two individuals

Experiential intimacy: Intimacy developed by personal experiences with the other.

Freedom from Vs Freedom to: Freedom from other people/agencies is independence whereas freedom to is psychological autonomy.

Honest communication: Free and open communication with the other without any ulterior motivation.

Hostility: Negative feelings towards self or to others resulting in depreciation of positive values.

Independent: The condition of being free from the control of others; it is freedom from others and not freedom to take one's own decisions and actions.

Intimacy: Physical and mental proximity between two individuals with emotional bond and readiness to share all experiences with the other without any inhibition and reservations.

Knowledge intimacy: Relationship between two individuals purely in terms of sharing of ideas without any reservation.

Psychological Autonomy: Freedom to take one's own decisions and actions without any anxiety or fear.

Psychological Dependency: Tendency to cling on to others for comforts and security. The person feels helpless in the absence of approval and appreciation from the other person.

Romantic intimacy: Intimacy between men and women who are in love with each other.

Self esteem: Positive attitude towards oneself; tendency to look at the positive side of oneself.

Submissive: Being compliant and obedient to others.

References:

Cook, W.W and Medley, D.M. (1954).,

"Proposed hostility and pharisaic-virtue scale for the MMPI".

J. Appl. Psychology, 1954, 38, 414-418.

Fromm, Erich. (1994).,

Escape from Freedom

New York: Holt.

Fromm, Erich. (2013).,

The Anatomy of Human Destructiveness

New York: Open Road Media.

Fromm, Erich. (2022).,

Fear of Freedom

U.K.: Taylor and Francis (T&F).

Grey, John. (2005).,

Men are from Mars, Women are from Venus

New York: Harper Collins.

Konrad, Lorenz. (1974).,

On Aggression

New York: Harper paper backs.

Malandro, Loretta. (2014).,

Speak Up, Show Up and Stand Out: The 9 Communication Rules You Need to Succeed

U.S.A./U.K.: McGraw-Hill Professional.

Murphy, Judy. (2011).,

Assertiveness: How to Stand Up for Yourself and Still Win the Respect of Others.

Great Escape Independent Publishing Platform.

Navran, L. (1954).,

"A rationally derived MMPI scale to measure dependence".

J. Consult. Psychology, 1954, 18, 192.

Paterson, R.J. (2022).,

The Assertiveness Workbook: How to Express Your Ideas and Stand Up for Yourself at Work and Relationships.

Aukland: New Harbinger Publications.

Potter, Daniel. (2020).,

Aggressive Behaviour

California: Daniel Potter Institute.

Ringer, Robert. (1984).,

Winning through Intimidation

Minnesota: Fawcett: Reissue Edition.

Ryan, R.M. and Deci, E.L. (2017).,

Self Determination Theories: Basic Psychological Needs in Motivation, Development and Wellness.

New York City: The Guilford Press.

Chapter 7

Social Relations and leadership Role

How do we attain Happiness with Success?

Step-2: Be sociable and ready to take up leadership role in groups

Human beings are social beings, under the influence and control of other human beings. This condition implies that a person needs the physical or psychological presence of others for his/her own survival and growth. Deprivation of this need may result in some behaviour deviation affecting mental health. Capacity for healthy and appropriate social interaction with a group of persons is necessary for successful leadership.

There are two personal attributes associated with social leadership.

(1) Social extroversion and (2) Leadership role in social groups.

Social Extroversion / Introversion:

The social extroversion is the mindset of involvement and participation in group activities and a prominent role of directing and controlling the group activities is leadership. The concepts 'Introversion' and 'Extroversion' are introduced in psychology by Carl Gustav Jung. Introversion means that the life energy of a person is spent on activities concerned with the thoughts and feelings of the person where as extroversion implies that the life energies are directed towards external matters. The introvert is not sociable, but, the extrovert is very sociable and outgoing personality. In this book, the measurement scale is social introversion and the social extroversion is the inverse of introversion. In the subscale from MMPI on social introversion developed by Drake (Drake, L.E. 1946), there were 70 items which were reduced to 27 by the four criteria mentioned under chapter 5. By the criterion of discrimination index below 0.3, further rejection of 14 items was made. Now the items in the subscale are 13 in the abridged 92 statements test. The score distribution was found normal that enable us to adopt parametric statistical analysis. There are no statistical significant differences by gender, age and academic faculty background. The norm for interpretation, therefore, is the same for all categories of respondents. Reliability and validity indices are well above 0.70. Correlations of social extroversion with other personal attributes as follows: Strong (above 0.70): Autonomy and leadership; Moderate (0.50-0.70), Self esteem, Regard for others, teaching potentiality and counsellor personality.

findings on social introversion and extroversion: Introverts can be converted into extroverts by more social engagements; extroversion is more pronounced among the transactional leaders than among the transformational leaders. Empathy and free interactions are more pronounced among the extroverts engaged in the service sector (Helgoe. Laurie. 2013; Covey, S.R. 1989; Loehken, silvia 2015).

Leadership role in groups:

Leadership role is defined as setting objectives, directing, controlling and motivating the group to attain the goals. The subscale on leadership developed by Gough (Gough, H.G. 1957) was used for the purpose. There were 50 items in the original scale and this was reduced to 23 by the accepted criteria and further reduced to 15 by the criterion of rejection by discrimination index.

The score distribution was found normal for the creation of norms in percentile of the z-scores. There was no significant difference of age, gender and academic faculty background of the respondents. Therefore, the same norm can be applied to all the subgroups. There is strong correlation of leadership with Psychological autonomy, Social extroversion, and Teaching potentiality. The association is moderate with Intimacy, Self esteem, Regard for others and Counsellor personality. Acceptability of the scale is strong as the reliability and validity correlation indices are above 0.80.

Important findings on Social extroversion and leadership:

Transformational leadership, in comparison with transactional leadership, is more effective in improving the performance of employees. Innovation and adaptability are the two main pillars of transformational leadership. Leaders who exhibit empathy by their listening to the ideas and feelings of the followers are associated well with the wellbeing of the employees. For the achievement of short term goals and conditions of emergencies, transactional leadership is found better than transformational leadership. Transactional leadership is found better under structured situations and routine mechanical nature of work of the employees. Lower employee turnover, higher job satisfaction and better team management are associated with emotional intelligence of the leader. Female democratic leaders are found more under the transformational leadership category (Rumsay, M.G. 2012; Grint, K 2010; Convey, S.R. 1989).

The combination effects of social extroversion and leadership role are depicted in the following figure:

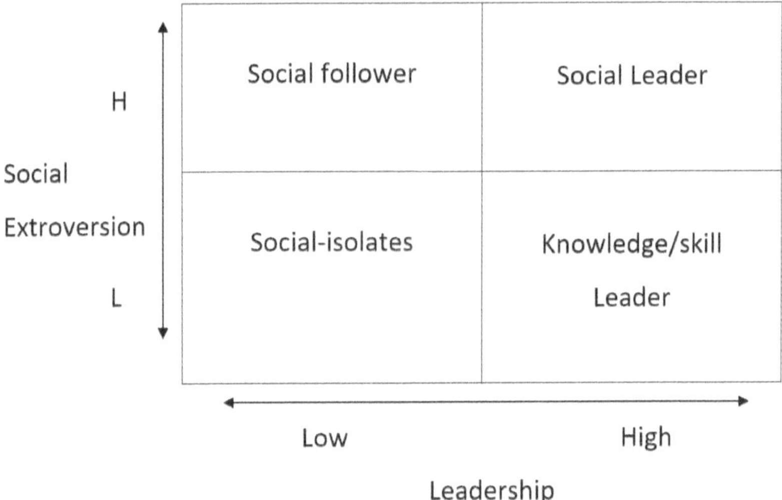

The figure given above is self explanatory. High leadership when combined with high social extroversion, it results in 'Social Leadership'; The consequence of high leadership with low social extroversion is the category of 'Knowledge/Skill Leadership'; High social extroversion without any leadership quality results in the category of 'Social Follower' and low both in leadership and extroversion is the category of 'Social Isolate' (Sylvia, Loehken 2015)

If you plan to attain happiness with success, you have to be a social leader or at least a social follower. Knowledge/Skill leader will be accepted well by the followers in a particular domain wherein an expert in the domain will be accepted as their leader within the limited scope.

There are many different types of leadership based on the nature of functions to be carried out by the group.

1. Entrepreneurial leadership with focus on taking initiative in organising something new.

2. Administrative leadership wherein the emphasis is on management of an institution/organization.

3. Political leadership wherein there is a struggle to dominate over the opponent, real or imagined. Another classification is transactional vs. transformational leadership wherein maintaining the status quo is an essential part of transactional leadership and introducing change for a better state of affairs is the essence of transformational leadership. Leadership is also classified in terms of the behavioural style of the leadership — Authoritarian, democratic and indifferent types. Each style has its own advantage and limitations based on three factors. The nature of work, the nature of the situation and the nature of the followers are the three factors that influence the effectiveness of the leadership styles.

(Grint, Keith. 2010; Rumsay, M.G. 2012; Covey, S.R. 1989).

Glossary of Terms:

Administrative leadership: Leadership to maintain the existing state of affairs with focus on direction and control.

Authoritarian style: A style of the leader characterised by forceful imposition of authority without any concern for the feeling of the followers.

Authoritative: an act of providing authentic (reliable and valid) information to the concerned.

Democratic style: A personal style of the leader in which the followers are given opportunities to participate in the decision making process.

Entrepreneurial leadership: Leadership with focus on starting something new in business or in other areas

Knowledge/skill leader: An acquired leadership by virtue of the expertise of the person either in knowledge or skill relevant to the attainment of the set goal of the group.

'Leave it as it is' style: The French equivalent to this word is 'Leissefaire' meaning that the person is not all interested in the affairs of group activities. He/she is there in the group by physical presence or by formal position that he/she holds and nothing else.

Political leadership: leadership to represent a group of people who do not have the power to influence the higher ups.

Social Extroversion: A socially outgoing personality wherein the life energy is spent on external matters than on self.

`**Social follower:** One who is active in all activities of a group, but does not take up the role of the group leader

Social introversion: A socially withdrawn type of behaviour wherein the life energy is concentrated on one's own internal thoughts and feelings.

Social isolate: One who is neither interested in the group activities by way of participation and involvement nor in leadership role of the group.

Social leader: One who is directing, controlling and motivating a group of people who are known as followers or subordinates.

Transactional leadership: leadership under structured work and organization wherein the role of the leader is to attain the short term goals.

Transformational leadership: Leadership for change and innovation with a view on long term goals.

References:

Covey, S.R. (1989).,

The 7 Habits of Highly Effective People

California: Free Press

Drake. L.C. (1946).,

"A social Introversion Extroversion Scale in the MMPI"

J. Applied Psychology, 1946, 30, 51-54.

Grint, Keith. (2010).,

Leadership: A Very Short Introduction

U.K.: Oxford University Press.

Gough, H.G. (1957).,

California Psychological Inventory Manual

Palo Alto: Consulting Psychologists Press.

Helgoe, Laurie. (2013).,

Introvert Power: Why your Inner Life is Your Hidden Strength.

2nd Edition

Illinois: Sourcebooks Inc.

Loehken, Silvia. (2015).,

The Power of Personality: How Introverts and Extroverts can Combine to Amazing Effect

London: John Murray Press.

Rumsey, M.G. ((Edr). (2012).,

The Oxford Handbook of Leadership

U.K: Oxford University Press.

Chapter 8

Life Positions

How to attain Happiness with Success?

Step 3: Adopt a life position, 'I am OK, You are OK'

Here the expression OK implies 'I am perfectly well with positive feelings' It is basically a positive attitude towards self and also towards others. There are two scales for the measurement of life positions.

1. Attitude towards self (Self esteem)

2. Attitude towards others (Regard for others). The assessment is already in positive form and so there is no need for an inversion. However, for better clarity, the term Self esteem is used for Attitude towards self, and the term Regard for others is for attitude towards others.

Both these scales are developed by Gibson, (Gibson, R.L. 1955). The scale on Attitude towards Self had 20 items and this was reduced to 8 items by the rejection criteria. There was no rejection by the discrimination index. The score distribution was found normal that permitted applications of parametric statistical analysis. The norm is applicable to all categories as there is no significant difference with reference to gender, age and academic faculty background of the respondents.

Reliability and validity are at the acceptance level. Correlations of this trait (Self esteem) with other personal attributes are as follows: No strong correlations with other traits; Moderate correlations with psychological Autonomy, Intimacy, Social Extroversion, Leadership, Teaching Potentiality and Counsellor Personality; The scale on Attitude towards others was also developed by Gibson (Gibson, R.L. 1955) This scale had 20 items and it was reduced to 7 items by the common criteria. All the 7 items showed acceptance level of discrimination index and so no item was rejected by this criterion.

The score distribution was found normal and the same norm can be applied for score interpretations as there is no significant difference among Gender, age, and academic faculty background. Reliability and validity indices were found above 0.70. Correlations with other personality attributes are as follows: Strong correlations: nil; Moderate correlations: Intimacy, social introversion, Leadership, Teaching potentiality, and Counsellor Personality.

Some research findings on Self esteem/Attitude towards self:

There is a need to make distinction between Self esteem and narcissism (Vaknin, S. 2015). Self esteem is positively associated with mental health whereas narcissism has a negative connotation in mental health. Self esteem of children and adolescents are highly influenced by parental relationship (Gottman, J. 2007). Income and the economic status are related to self esteemed—better the economic status, higher is the self esteem; nature of work/profession will influence the level of self esteem. Higher level of self esteem is an intrinsic motivational factor in social and professional life (Branden, N. 1994; Goleman, D. 2020)

Some research findings on Regard for others:

Regard for others is associated with empathetic emotions -- People with high regard for others have a special gift of understanding the emotions of others (McLaren, Karla. 2013; Krznaric, Roman. 2015). Interpersonal space gets reduced by higher levels of regard for others; cordial interpersonal relationship is the outcome of reduced interpersonal space. (Hall, E.T. 1990; Sommer, Robert 1969).

The combined effect of Self esteem and Regard for others is shown in the following figure:

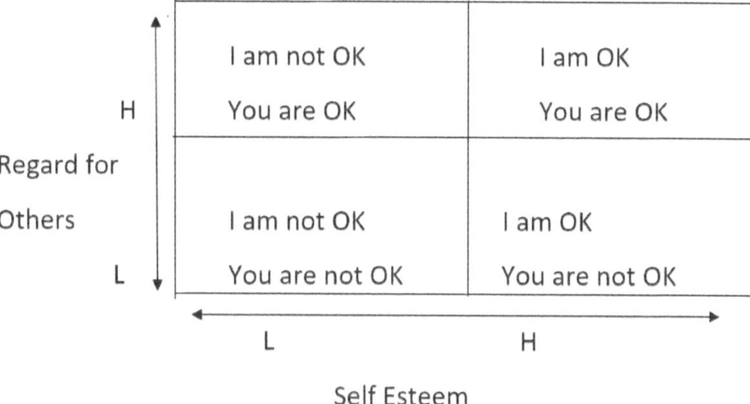

The figure given above shows the combination effect in four segments:

1. Top left corner is the first category, I am not Ok, but you are OK implying low self esteem and high regard for others. This is the first early experience of the child with the feeling that the self is helpless and others (grown up people) are Ok.

2. Just below that category on the bottom left is the life position of I am not Ok, you are also not OK implying low self esteem and low regard for others. This is the second stage of development where the person perceives the inadequacies of the person conceived as OK at the first stage.

3. The right side bottom depicts the life position of I am OK, but you are not OK and this third level outcome of the life position is evident during adolescent and the youth periods.

4. The top right hand box shows highly positive life position of I am OK, You are OK. This is the 4th and last stage of development in interpersonal relations.

The second stage category at the bottom left is the most negative one -- I am not OK and you are also not OK. These are the life position of a person and not the structural, functional and other important concepts of Transactional Analysis school of thoughts of Eric Burne. Discussion of the entire spectrum of Transactional Analysis may require another volume and so that part is excluded in this section. Impacts of the four categories of mind set are as follows:

I am not OK, you are OK:

This first stage of development starts with helplessness in the midst of other human adults. Karen Horney called this stage as basic anxiety of every one which is to be overcome in due course as healthy matured adult. The description of behaviour of this type is somewhat similar to 'moving towards people' (Horney, K. 1937)

There are many books on transactional Analysis clarifying the concepts, theories and practices which are not discussed in this book. (Berne, Eric 1961.,1996., McCormic, P. 1970); Hall, E.T. 1990; McCormic, P. 1970).

I am Not OK, You are not OK: At this second stage of development, attitude toward self and also towards others are negative by the perception of negative attributes of the interacting persons.

I am OK, You are not OK:

In this life position the person at the third stage, the person assumes the role of a superior being and takes a dominant role in interpersonal relations and often such a role may prove dysfunctional. The fate of the authoritarian dominant leader awaits them in the long run. A person of this type may win a battle, but will lose the war in the long run. (Horney, K. 1937)

I am OK, You are OK: A person reaches at this final stage when he is matured with personal experience of working together with positive feelings for both self and others. This stage of development is an indication of good mental health with a sense of wellbeing.

(Harris, T.A. 1995; Amy B. H.T. and Harris, T.A. 1995; Horney, K. 19 McLaren, K. 2013; Schein, E.H. 2011 Krznaric, R. 2015; Volkanin, S. 2015; Jeffrey, E.Y. and Janet. S.K. 1994).

Glossary of Terms:

I am ok, you are ok: High self esteem for self and high esteem for others

I am ok, you are not ok: High self esteem and low esteem for others

I am not ok, you are ok: Low self esteem and high regard for others

I am not ok, you are not ok: Low esteem for self and others

Attitude towards others: High or low positive attitude Toward other people

Attitude towards self: High or low positive attitude towards oneself; self esteem

Crossed transactions: Misunderstanding in communication when one acts from one ego state and the other responds from another ego state.

Ego states: Three style of acting and responding in interpersonal transactions i.e. the Child Ego state, the Adult Ego state, and the Parent Ego state. The child ego state is further classified into three categories i.e. the natural child, the manipulating child and the adopted child. Parent ego state is divided into the supportive parent and the controlling parent.

Games people play: Transactions among people that results in giving strokes for personal pleasure or with an ulterior motive of belittling the other.

Life positions: The OK feelings in life with respect to self and others

Parallel transactions: Complementary transactions with positive feelings for both parties. From a child ego state to a parental ego state and vice versa or an adult to adult transaction is a parallel transaction

Regard for others: Mind set to perceive the good qualities of other people; positive view of others with appreciation towards other people; appreciation of the positive side of others; regard for the other.

Self esteem: a mindset of perceiving the positive side of oneself; self appreciation; love and regard for oneself

Strokes: feedbacks one gives or receives during interpersonal interactions

Time structuring: How people spend their time when they are at work or otherwise? Work, past time, game, intimacy etc are examples.

Transactional Analysis: Name given to the school of thought developed by Eric Burne for understanding the behaviour—adjusted or maladjusted—of people in their interaction process.

Ulterior transactions: At the surface level of social interactions, it may look normal, but the interacting people know the hidden meanings of such words or actions of the other.

References:

Amy B. Harris and Thomas A. Harris. (1995).,

Staying OK

India: Arrow Books.

Berne, Eric. (1961).,

Transactional Analysis in Psychotherapy: A Systematic Individual and Social Psychiatry.

New Zealand: Castle Books.

Berne, Eric. (1996).,

Games People Play: The Psychology of Human Relationships

New York: Ballantine Books.

Branden, Nathaniel. (1994).,

The Six Pillars of Self Esteem

USA: Bentam Books.

Gibson, R.L. (1955).,

A Factor Analysis of measures change following Client Centred therapy.

Ph.D. Dissertation, Pennsylvania State University.

Goleman, Daniel. (2020).,

Emotional intelligence: Why It Can Matter More than I.Q.

UK: Bloomsbury Publishing.

Goleman, Daniel. (2007).,

Social Intelligence: The New Science of Human Relationships

UK: Arrow Books Ltd.

Gottman, John. (1997).,

Raising an Emotional Intelligent Child: The Heart of Parenting

New York: Simon &Schuster.

Hall, Edward T. (1990)

The hidden Dimension

USA: Anchor, Reissue Edn.

Horney, Karen. (1937).,

The Neurotic Personality of Our Time

New York: Norton.

Jeffrey E. Young and Janet S. Klosko. (1994).,

Reinventing Your Life: The Breakthrough Program to End Negative Behaviour and Feel Great Again

USA: Penguin Putnam.

Krznaric, Roman. (2015).,

Empathy: Why It Matters and How to Get It.

UK: Rider & Co.

McCormick, Paul. (1970).,

Introduce Yourself to Transactional Analysis – A TA Handbook

California: San Joaquin TA Study Group.

McLaren, Karla. (2013).,

The Art of Empathy: A Complete Guide to Life's Most Essential Skill.

Schein, E.H. (2011).,

Helping: How to Offer, Give, and Receive Help

Berrett Koehler.

Sommer, Robert. (1969).,

Personal Space: The Behavioural Basis of Design

NJ: Prentice Hall.

Thomas A. Harris. (1995).,

I'm OK, You're OK

UK: Arrow.

Vaknin, Sam. (2015).,

Malignant Self-Love: Narcissism Revisited

Narcissus Publications.

Chapter 9

Empathetic Communication

How to attain Happiness with success?

Step 4: communicate well with empathy

In Social interactions, communication is the most important factor closely followed by empathetic understanding of the other. (Ting-Toomey, S. 1999). The two tests developed for the purpose are:

1. Teaching potentiality

2. Counsellor personality

Teaching Potentiality/Communication:

The scale on teaching potentiality was developed by Gowan and Gowan (1955) with 98 items which was reduced to 18 items by the major rejection criteria. Five items were further rejected by the discrimination index. The score distribution was found normal. Differences by age, gender, and academic faculty background were found not significant and hence the same norm can be applied to all groups. Reliability and validity meet the standard for acceptance.

Correlations of teaching potentiality with other traits are as follows:

Strong correlations are with psychological autonomy, leadership and counsellor personality; moderate association with intimacy, social extroversion, self esteem and regard for others.

Counsellor Personality/Empathetic understanding of the other:

Another scale of measurement is counsellor personality wherein the focus is on empathy for better relationship. This test developed by Cottle and Penny ((Cottle, W.L and Penny, M.M. 1954) had 51 MMPI items. This number was reduced to 17 items with further rejection of 5 items making it a 12 item scale in the short form of MMPI for the Indian respondents. The score distribution is normal for the application of parametric statistical analysis. Differences among the subgroups such as age, gender, and academic faculty background of the respondents were not statistically significant and so the same norm can be applied for interpretations of the scores. Reliability and validity were found acceptable as they are above 0.70 levels. Positive association with other traits are as follows:

Strong correlation: Intimacy and teaching potentiality, moderate – Psychological autonomy, Social extroversion, Leadership, Self esteem and regard for others.

The combination effect of teaching potentiality and counsellor personality is depicted in the following figure:

	L	H
H	Good Listener, but Poor Speaker	Good speaker & Empathetic Listener
Empathy (Counsellor Personality) L	Poor Speaker & Poor Listener	Good Speaker, but Poor Listener

Communication (Teaching Potentiality)

Enhancement of happiness with success is possible when effective communication is combined with empathetic feeling towards the other.

Good communication without empathy, though impressive at the initial stage, may make the person ineffective in interpersonal relations in the long run. Empathy without good communication is similar to a person who is liked by others, but incompetent in producing the desired results. And the fourth level combination resulting poor communication and poor empathy is like an unimpressive and ineffective person.

Research findings on empathy and communication:

There are two types of empathy: cognitive empathy in understanding the perspective of the other and affective empathy of sharing the emotion of the other; Experiencing the same emotion as that of the other creates an emotional bond between the two; securing attachment at the early period of life fosters empathetic skills. Empathy is positively associated with pro-social behaviour of the person concerned which in turn is integral part of interpersonal relations; Absence of empathetic feelings is associated with mental illness such as autism, psychopath etc. Empathy is a leverage to enhance social cohesion and mental health. ((Rogers, C.R. 1995); Derald, W.S. and David Sue. 2008; Staemmler, F.M 2011; Eagan, Gerald 2020).

Clear and concise message reduces misunderstanding and enhances comprehension; Training in active listening is associated with better interpersonal relations and better conflict resolution; Cultural sensitivity and language barriers are to be considered when we study psycho-social differences in communication. (Brownell, J. 2013; Ting-Toomey, S. 1999; Hocker, J.M. and Wilmot, W.W. 2014; Bradberry, T. And Greaves, J. 2009)

Glossary of Terms:

Communication: The process of arriving at common understanding by verbal and non verbal means

Counsellor personality: The psychological characteristics of a person who is trying to help and support one who is mentally or otherwise sick and helpless.

Empathy: The condition of common emotion between the two interacting persons

Empathetic communicator: one who is communicating with empathetic feelings.

Non empathetic communicator: one who is good at communicating but poor in his/her empathetic feelings.

Non communicative empathiser: One good in empathy but poor in communication

Non communicating non empathiser: A person who is neither good in communication nor in empathy.

Teaching potentiality: Psychological factors associated with successful teaching, formal or informal, i.e. Effective communication and good understanding of the relevant subjects of communication.

References:

Bradberry, T., & Greaves, J. (2009).,

Emotional intelligence

California: TalentSmart.

Brownell, J. (2013).,

Listening: Attitudes, principles, and skills.

New York: Pearson Higher Ed.

Cottle, W.CL and Penny, M.M. (1954)

"Personal Characteristics of Counsellors:III. An Experimental Scale".

J. Counsel. Psychology, 1954, 1, 74-77.

Derald Wing Sue and David Sue. (2008).,

Counselling the Culturally Diverse: Theory and Practice. 5th Ed

New Jersey: John Wiley and Sons.

Egan, Gerald (2020).,

The Skilled Helper: A Problem-Management and Opportunity-Development Approach to Helping. 11th Ed.

Delhi: Cengage India Pvt, Ltd.

Gowan, J.C. and Gowan, M.S. (1955).,

"A Teacher Prognosis scale for the MMPI"

J. Educ. Res. 1955, 49, 1-12.

Hocker, J. L., & Wilmot, W. W. (2014).,

Interpersonal conflict.

New York: McGraw-Hill Education.

Rogers, C.R. (1995).,

On Becoming a Person: A Therapist's View of Psychotherapy. 2nd Ed.

New York: Harper One.

Staemmler, F.M. (2011).,

Empathy in Psychotherapy: How Therapists and Clients Understand Each Other

Germany: Springer Publishing Co.

Ting-Toomey, S. (1999).,

Communicating across cultures.

New York: Guilford Press.

Chapter 10

Proactive Behaviour

How to attain happiness with success?

Step-5: Be a proactive person in your cognitive and emotive behaviour.

Proactive means a response and not a reaction. Reaction is involuntary and spontaneous, as a push of the past, whereas a response is a voluntary decision with due consideration for the future—a pull of the future. There are two components in such proactive behaviour: the cognitive part of task performance, problem solving and decision making and the emotional part in terms of time taken for decisions and actions. Here, in this text, two scales of measurements are used; one for the measurement of decisiveness (the inverse of Immaturity) and the other on self control (the inverse of impulsivity).

Decisiveness:

Scale for the measurement of emotional immaturity was developed by Pearson (1954) with 48 items from MMPI. This number was reduced to 14 by the criteria mentioned and a further reduction of 3 items by discrimination index. The final number of items in the revised subscale is thus 11 only.

The score distribution adheres to the bell shaped normal distribution and norm for interpretation from this normal distribution was made applicable to all except the female 26 years and above group. However, one may note that Age group 26 years and above is different from the younger group. This observation leads to the conclusion that maturity of female members 26 years and above is superior to the male members, though there was no such significant difference at the earlier period. In the strict sense, there is a need for a separate norm for the 26 years and above female respondents. Validity and reliability is above the acceptance level. Correlation coefficients of the decisive scale with other scales are as follows: All the correlations with other traits are very weak, indicating that the trait decisiveness is a separate entity from others.

Important findings: Decisiveness is positively associated with hopefulness among university students; Decisiveness can enhance the overall wellbeing condition of the person; Emotional instability fostered by immaturity and impulsivity can affect the decision making process. (Johnson, S. 2018.; Gladwell, M. 2005.; Duke, Annie. 2018.; Heath, C and Heath D. 2013.; Kahneman, Daniel. 2015.).

Self Control:

The second subscale relevant to proactive behaviour is self control, the inverse of impulsivity. This test was developed by Gough (1957) with 21 items from MMPI. This was reduced to 8 without any rejection by discrimination index. Score distribution was found normal. There was no significant differences between male and female respondents; no significant difference among academic faculty background; but the group above 26 years was found to be different from the younger age group and it leads to the conclusion that people generally become more self controlled or less impulsive when they cross 25 years. A separate norm was required for interpretation of scores for the age group 26 years and above. Reliability and validity indices are above 0.70 levels and so it is above the acceptable level. Correlation coefficients with other traits are weak indicating that this trait is different from others.

Important findings: self controlled actions are generally properly conceived with due care for the risk element and appropriate to the situation; individuals with high score in self control show lower rash actions and better emotional stability; effective parenting with emotional attachment leads to higher level of self control; effective intervention strategies such as yoga, mindfulness, cognitive behaviour therapy etc are useful in controlling impulsivity and thereby enhancing self control.(Mischel, Walter. 2015.; Neff, Krish. 2015.; Dweck, C.S. 2006.; McGonigal, Kelly. 2013).

The combination effect of Decisiveness and self control is depicted in the following figure:

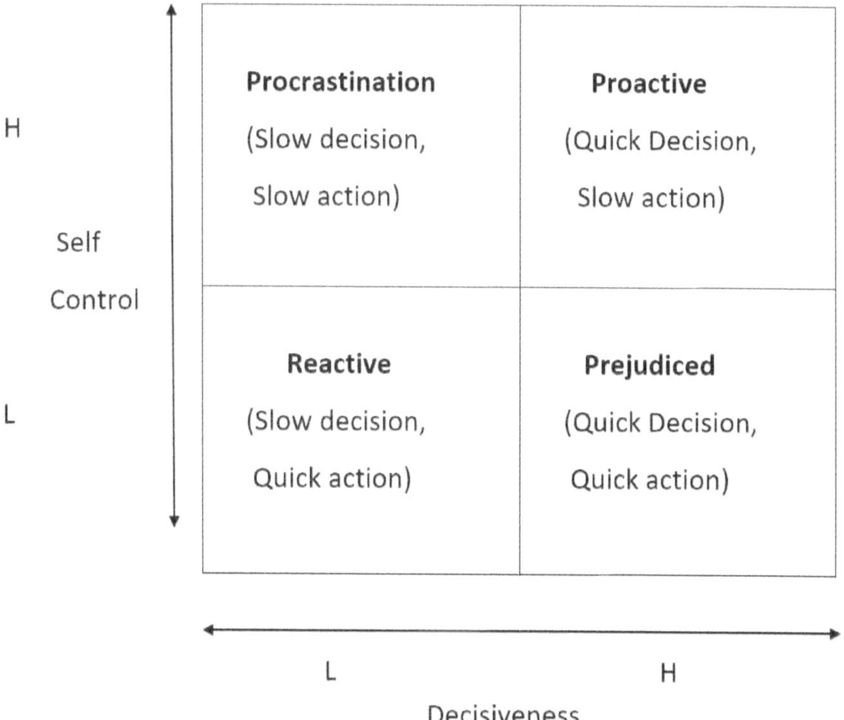

The above figure shows the impacts of the speed of taking decision and the speed if implementing that decision. Quick decision and slow action means proactive and the opposite slow decision and quick action is reactive indicating high emotionality. Slow decision and slow action is an indication of procrastination. Quick decision and quick action means that the decision is not the result of a response, it is rather reaction based some convictions formed earlier from his/her own experience i.e. prejudiced.

It may be noted that the general advice that one may take his own time for taking a decision, but be quick in its implementation is not supported in this study. Rather, the advice is to be the opposite: be quick in decision but slow in action to review the decision taken. This proactive behaviour will take away the barrier created by irrational emotions.

Proactive: The synergic effect of the combination of decisiveness and self control is the proactive behaviour i.e. a meaningful and useful response rather than a reaction by the push of the past. It leads to personal efficacy and work satisfaction. Proactive behaviour fosters positive outcomes in team management. A meaningful job reinforces proactive behaviour which in turn provides more meaningfulness. Enhanced wellbeing, better task performance, problem solving and decision making are the positive consequences of this proactive category of behaviour. (Parker, S.K and Bindl, U. 2017; Cremer, D.D. and Thianamen Zang 2013.; DuBrin, A. J. 2013.; Covey. S.R. 1990; Goleman, D. 1995).

Prejudiced: This category of quick reaction is based on the conviction that 'I know everything and so I need not think further on the problem.' Prejudice is preconceived notion or prejudgement without waiting for logical evidences to prove or disprove the conviction. Bias, stereotypes, and absence of tolerance to diversities are the outcome of such prejudiced reactions. It is dysfunctional to mental health and progress in life. (Banji, M.R and Greenmal, A.G. 2016.; Howard, J.R. 2014.;)

Reactive: It is the opposite of proactive. Highly emotional type people are generally quick in action, but slow in decision. The indecisive state of mind often forces to quick action for an immediate relief which in turn creates a feeling of repentance for not taking the right decision. (David, Susan. 2016.; Duhigg, Charles. 2014.; Kahneman, Daniel. 2015.; Goleman, Daniel. 1995.)

Procrastination: Postponement of both decision and action is the essence of procrastination. 'To be or not to be' of a doubting Thomas is the hallmark of this category of people and this in turn creates a paralysis of action. (Steel, Piers. 2012.; Pychyl, T.A. 2013.; Ludwig, P and Schicker, A. 2019.; Burka, J.B and Yuen, L.M. 2008).

Only proactive behaviour leads to better mental health conducive to well adjustment to the demands of the changing environment.

Glossary of Terms:

Decision making: Decision making and problem solving have the same process, but they differ at the final stage; In problem solving the selected alternatives are the solutions to the problem and so it is called the right alternative. In decision making, the alternative selected is the best one among the available; other alternatives not selected is time consuming, less efficient, and more costly.

Prejudiced: Preconceived notions about something resulting in quick decision and quick action.

Problem solving: A problem is the perceived gap between what is and what it should be; after generating a number of alternatives, the person has to select one of the alternatives as a solution to the problem.

Procrastination: The tendency or behaviour disposition characterised by postponement – prolonged time in decision making and its implementation.

Proactive: Cognitive and emotive disposition that is healthy for achieving the desired results

Reactive: A condition of slow decision and quick actions that is likely to generate emotional behaviour and feelings.

Task performance: Work to be done within a stipulated time and other conditions.

References:

Banaji, M.R. and. Greenwald, A.G. (2016).,

Blindspot: Hidden Biases of Good People

New York: Random House.

Burka, Jane B. and. Yuen, L.M. (2008).,

Procrastination: Why You Do It, What to Do About It Now

Boston: De Capo Lifelong Books.

Covey, S.R. (1990).,

The 7 Habits of Highly Effective People: Powerful Lessons in Personal Change.

California: Free Press.

Cremer, D.D, and Tiananmen Zhang. (2013).,

The Proactive Leader: How to Overcome Procrastination and Be a Bold Decision-Maker

London: Palgrave Macmilian.

David, Susan. (2016).,

Emotional Agility: Get Unstuck, Embrace Change, and Thrive in Work and Life

New York: Avery.

DuBrin A.J. (2013).,

Proactive Personality and Behaviour for Individual and Organizational Productivity

U.K: Edward Elgar Publishing Ltd.

Duhigg, Charles. (2014).,

The Power of Habit: Why We Do What We Do in Life and Business

New York: Random House.

Duke, Annie. (2018)

Thinking in Bets: Making Smarter Decisions When You Don't Have All the Facts

Penguin Group (USA): Portfolio Division.

Dweck, Carol. S. (2006).,

Mindset: The New Psychology of Success

New York: Random House Publishing.

Gladwell, Malcolm. (2005).,

Blink: The Power of Thinking Without Thinking

Boston: Back Bay Books; Little Brown.

Goleman, Daniel. (1995)

Emotional Intelligence: Why It Can Matter More Than IQ

New Delhi: Bloomsbury Publishing, India Pvt. Ltd.

Gough. H.C. (1957).,

California Psychological Inventory Manual

Palo Alto: Consulting Psychologists Press.

Heath, Chip and Heath, Dan. (2013).,

Decisive: How to Make Better Choices in Life and Work

New York: Crown Business.

Howard J. Ross. (2014).,

Everyday Bias: Identifying and Navigating Unconscious Judgments in Our Daily Lives

Maryland: Rowman & Littlefield.

Johnson, Steven. (2018).,

Farsighted: How We Make the Decisions That Matter the Most

New York: Riverhead Books.

Kahneman, Daniel. (2015).,

Thinking, Fast and Slow

U.K.: Penguin.

Ludwig Petr and Schicker, Adela. (2019)

End of Procrastination: How to Stop Postponing and Live a Fulfilled Life.

Sydney: Murdoch Books.

McGonigal, Kelly. (2013).,

The Willpower Instinct: How Self-Control Works, Why It Matters, and What You Can Do to Get More of It.

New York: Avery.

Mischel, Walter. (2015).,

The Marshmallow Test: Why Self-Control Is the Engine of Success

London: Corgi Books.

Neff, Krish. (2015).,

Self-Compassion: The Proven Power of Being Kind to Yourself.

New York: William Morrow.

Parker, S.K and Bindl, U.K. (Edr). (2017).,

Proactivity at Work: Making Things Happen in Organizations.

U.K.: Routledge.

Pearson, J. S. (1954).,

Psychometric correlation of Emotional Immaturity

Ph.D, Dissertation, University of Minnesota.

Pychyl, Timothy A. (2013).,

Solving the Procrastination Puzzle: A Concise Guide to Strategies for Change

New York: Tarcher Perigee.

Steel, Piers. (2012).,

The Procrastination Equation: How to Stop Putting Things Off and Start Getting Stuff Done

New York: Harper Perennial.

Chapter 11

The Concept of Personal Efficacy

In the earlier chapters (from 6th to 10th chapters), the focus was on the measurement of 10 traits or personal qualities., in 5 pairs. The synergetic effects of combinations of two traits at a time from among these 5 pairs of 10 traits were also discussed in detail. To repeat, the pairs of traits are as follows: Pair No. 1: Psychological autonomy and Intimacy leading to four different types of behaviour pattern Viz., Assertive, Dominative, Submissive and Aggressive behaviour in interpersonal relations; Pair No. 2: Social extroversion and Leadership leading to the synergetic effect of social leadership, knowledge/Skill leadership, Social follower and Social isolates. Pair No. 3: Self esteem and regard for others leading to four types of life positions Viz., I am NOT OK, You are OK., I am NOT OK, You are NOT OK., I am OK, You are NOT OK., and the final development stage of I am OK and you are OK., Pair No. 4: Teaching Potentiality(communication) and Counselling Personality (Empathy) combination leading to Good communicator with empathetic understanding of the other, Good speaker, but not a listener, An empathetic non- communicator and the non-empathetic non- communicator are other categories. The final pair No. 5: Decisiveness and Self control leading to the synergetic four behaviour pattern Viz., The Proactive, the Prejudiced, the Reactive and the Procrastination types. From the studies, we have come to the conclusion that an assertive social leader with a I am OK, you are OK life position, an effective communicator with empathy and a proactive type person is likely to experience psychological wellness, or sreyas (happiness with success), the positive side of mental health.

The ten personality traits mentioned above are overt exhibited behaviour traits. Is it possible to reduce the number of traits based on the commonality among them? Yes, very much. The statistical method of Factor Analysis precisely aims at such reduction. High correlations among psychological autonomy, intimacy, social extroversion, leadership, Self esteem, Regard for others, Teaching potentiality and Counsellor Personality, imply a latent factor extracted from the commonness. A name is to be given for this latent factor. All these traits are related to interpersonal and social relations. We may give to this common factor, a name 'People Oriented mindset'. Decisiveness and Self control are outside this common factor as the correlations of these two traits with other 8 traits were found to be weak. However, the correlation between decisiveness and self control though not very strong is found to be moderate for making another set of factors. Cognitive and emotive components of this factor such as 'Performance oriented mindset', Task performance, problem solving, decision making and the time factor associated with them makes this latent factor by the name 'Performance orientation'.

The synergetic effect of the combination of 'people orientation' and 'performance orientation':

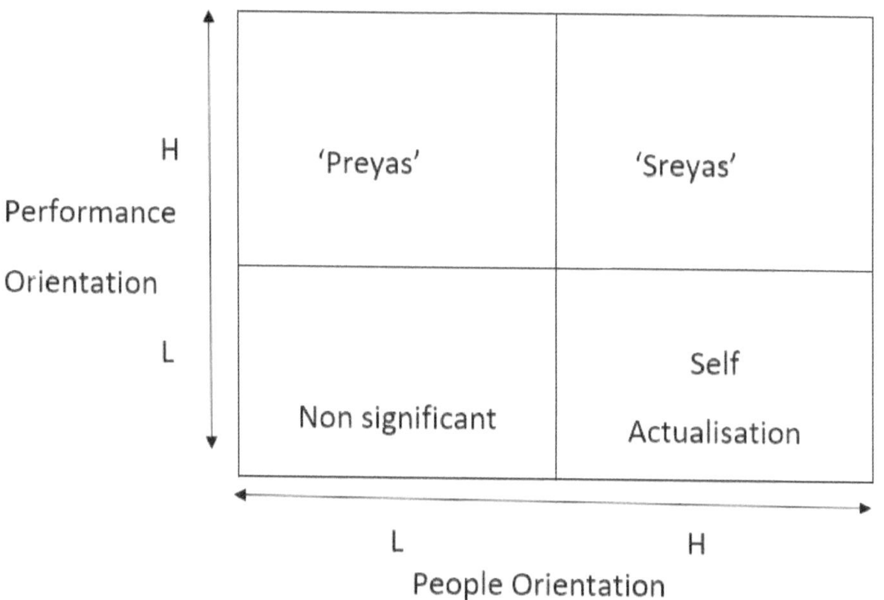

I. *'Sreyas'* i.e. Happiness with success; Effective and efficient persons with social values experience this state; Such people are executives/ managers/ administrators.

II. *'Preyas'* i.e. A category of People who are successful, but without much sustained happiness --Sustainability by their adherence to social and ethical norms and values; Staff specialists without work teams as subordinates may be of this category.

III. **'The Self Actualizing Person'** i.e. people who are doing certain things for its own sake without expecting any reward/award; Such people are happy, but may not be successful in attaining positions and possessions; Social workers, politicians without any administrative responsibility etc may belong to this category.

IV. **'The unknown insignificant persons'** by their ineffective and inefficient performance and maladjustment in interpersonal and social relations.

The figure given above assumes two measurement scales. But, it was already mentioned that these two attributes (People orientation and Performance orientation) are latent factors derived by factor analysis and not by measurement scales. However, we can create required scales from the measurable attributes responsible for the derived factors. Each trait such as psychological autonomy, intimacy etc. was categorized into five groups as follows: (1) Poor for the scores below 20th percentile; (2) Below average for the scores in between 20th and 40th percentile; (3) Average for the scores in between 40th and 60th percentile; (4) Above average for the scores in between 60th and 80th percentile and (5) Superior above the 80th percentile scores. These rank scores of 1 to 5 for each trait measured may be taken as a basis for the measurement of the derived factors. For the People Orientation scale find the average score values of 8 traits and convert it to a manageable number by a multiplication by a constant of 10. Similarly for the measurement of Performance orientation, take the average of two scales associated with the factor, convert the score into a manageable number by multiplication of a constant 10. The figure depicting the four categories of personal efficacy is possible only by such a device.

A combination of the people orientation and performance orientation is the real index of Personal efficacy. (Gladwell, M. 2008; Brenden, B. 2018; Ericsson, A. and Pool, Robert 2016 Kellis. 2013).

We are more familiar with the word 'Self efficacy' popularised by the research work of Albert Bandura (1997). Self efficacy is defined as self confidence in certain specific domain and it is not a generic term to cover many areas at the same time. Is self efficacy and personal efficacy one and the same? No. The scope of self efficacy is limited to a specific domain such as academic, sports, social work etc., whereas the scope of personal efficacy is wider to encompass the disposition of the person to be bold, courageous and confident in facing most of the unfamiliar and unstructured situations in life. (Duckworth, A. 2016). Here we have to clarify the meaning of the term 'Efficacy'. Achievement of the desired goal (effectiveness) with efficiency (economy in time, efforts and utilization of resources) and with adherence to social and ethical norms and values for sustainability is the idea covered by the term 'Personal Efficacy'.

Personal efficacy is the synergetic product of the combination of people orientation and performance orientation factors. (Keller, G. And Papasan, J. 2013). Low level of personal efficacy will lead to low level of Happiness with success and conversely high level of personal efficacy leads to high level of happiness with success. Happiness with success is the intersection of two areas, Happiness and success. Happiness with success implies success with happiness as they are overlapping in the intersection. This area of happiness with success is the area of 'Sreyas'. The area outside this intersection on the success side is 'Preyas'—success in terms of positions and possessions without happiness and sustainability in the long run. The area outside the intersection area on the 'happiness without success' is self actualization—doing something for its own sake without expecting any reward or award. In short, this book is on the psychology of 'Sreyas' or the Psychology of Personal Efficacy or the psychology of Happiness with Success. The following figure depicts the relationship among 'Sreyas', 'Preyas' and 'Self actualization'

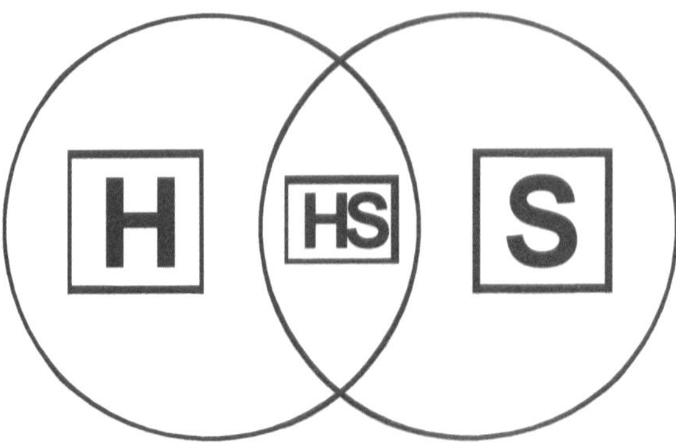

H. Happiness without any concern for award/rewards area under the Happiness circle (SELF ACTUALIZATION)

S. Success without long run sustained happiness under the Success circle ('PREYAS)

HS. Happiness with Success under the intersection area of the two circles (SREYAS).

Glossary of Terms:

People orientation: Concern and consideration for people in all situations in life.

Performance orientation: Concern and consideration for the work to be accomplished, including task performance, problem solving and decision making.

Personal efficacy: Belief of a person that he has the courage and confidence to adjust well in unfamiliar and unstructured situations in life. This term is more generic than specific as mentioned in self efficacy

'Preyas': This is a condition of being happy and successful for a shorter period on attaining possessions and positions in life. When this condition is made sustained for longer period by adherence to efficiency and social and ethical norms and values, then it transforms into 'Sreyas'.

Self actualization: A condition of doing activities for its own sake, without expecting any award or reward.

Self efficacy: Belief of a person that he/she has the courage and confidence to meet the challenges paused in a particular domain. It is specific to a particular field.

'Sreyas': This is a condition of being happy and successful in life. It is sustained thoughts and feelings and not a transient one.

References:

Bandura, A. (1997).,

Self-Efficacy: The Exercise of Control

New York: W.H. Freeman & Co.

Brendon Burchard. (2018).,

High Performance Habits: How Extraordinary People Become That Way

Delhi: Hay House India.

Duckworth, Angela. (2016).,

Grit: The Power of Passion and Perseverance

New York: Scribner.

Ericsson, Anders and Pool, Robert. (2016).,

Peak: Secrets from the New Science of Expertise

Boston: Houghton Mifflin Harcourt.

Gladwell, Malcolm. (2008).,

Outliers: The Story of Success

New York: Little, Brown & Co.

Keller, Gary and Papasan, Jay. (2013).,

The One Thing: The Surprisingly Simple Truth Behind Extraordinary Results

London: Hodder and Stoughton.

Chapter 12

Epilogue

In addition to the prime factors discussed in this book, there are some other factors that may contribute to 20% in personal efficacy/ happiness with success. They are (1) Attention to details (2) Tolerance to diversities (3) Language fluency (4) Time management (5) Urban sophistication (6) Knowledge/ skill in the specialization domain (7) General knowledge and current affairs to be at home in any social situation. The first three areas are indirectly covered in personal efficacy, but more detailed work is required for specific measurements. The remaining areas are better assessed by personal interview.

Now a question one may ask after reading this book: How do we improve personal efficacy from low level to high level? Reading a book or listening to a motivational speech may increase your knowledge on the subject, but may not improve the actual behaviour. The steps required for the expected change are: Unlearning of the existing thoughts, feelings and behaviour that hinder the new learning for providing enough space for change. The principles of unlearning are the same as that of learning. The change is only replacement of the existing one in favour of the desired attributes. (Brown, P.C. 2017; Kolb, D.A. 2014; Clear, J. 2018; Duhigg, C. 2014) This unlearning is possible only by new experiences. The 'mantra' for change is

'Expose yourself for your expansion'. Another 'Mantra' for change is 'Receive feedback for self corrections'. Knowledge alone is not sufficient for modification of behaviour, though it provides the required framework of concepts and theories. For skill development, the requirements are action learning through role play, modelling, and other methods. Such programmes are plenty, if individuals are willing to expose to such new experiences. Sensitivity training (Renuka Raj Sing. Et. al. 2022; Tuman, M.F. 2020);, Rational Emotive behaviour therapy (REBT) (Ellis, Albert, 1998). Behaviour Modification exercises (Miltenberger, R.G. 2015)). imitation of the desired change (Modelling) (Bandura A. 1969., 1997) N.L.P (Neuro -Linguistic Programme); Lindsey, A. 2010; Knight, Sue. 2002) etc. are some such training programmes. If such training programmes are to be successful, proper diagnosis for identification of the required change is a prerequisite. A training programme for the sake of training is meaningless. It should have a definite objectives and evaluation of the condition before and after programme to assess the effectiveness of the training programme.

Some further questions that you may ask at this juncture are: (1) Where are those 92 statements for you to respond for self improvement? (2) Is it possible for a thorough diagnosis of personality profile, so that you may identify areas of improvement in deficient areas? (3) Is it possible to change by training and if, 'yes' suggest some agencies who do such training programmes on the line suggested in this book.

Answers to these questions are as follows: Printing the 92 statements in this book is meaningless as nothing can be done with the statements alone without the keys, and standardised norms for interpretations. There are some technical and legal problems in providing complete details for diagnosis. Psychological tests are always under lock and key for avoiding possible misuse. On the question of training for personal development, the answer is there are too many training programmes and most of them are on communication (language fluency), urban sophistication, self presentation in interviews etc and not on the lines suggested in this book. For details on actual diagnosis and tailor made training programmes, I suggest that you may visit www.transformminds. com for obtaining full information on the test and training programmes or contact me personally for obtaining details on such information including actual conduct of the relevant personality efficacy.

My final words:

'Thank you for reading this book'

Glossary of Terms:

Behaviour Modification: Change in behaviour by conditioning/ deconditioning and other methods of learning.

Experiential learning: Learning by doing or participative involvement in Group activities/ projects.

Learning: Modification of behaviour by experience for habit formation

Modelling: Learning by imitation method for imbibing a desired behavioural dispositions/traits.

NLP: Neuro Linguistic Programming, as a method of training for the development of personality with focus on communication, urban sophistication, public relations etc.

REBT: Rational Emotive Behaviour Therapy with focus on changing perception of the individual or giving a new interpretation to an experience.

Sensitivity training: Explorations and explanations of behaviour exhibited by participant individuals in group by feedback mechanism. This type of training programme is also known as T-Group training

Unlearning: Modification of behaviour by experience to break a habit/ attitude for new learning

References:

Bandura, Albert. (1969).,

Principles of Behaviour Modification

New York: Holt, Rinehart and Winston.

Brown, P.C., Roediger, H.L III, and McDaniel, M.A. (2017).,

Make It Stick: The Science of Successful Learning.

Cambridge: Harvard University Press.

Clear, James. (2018).,

Atomic Habits: An Easy & Proven Way to Build Good Habits & Break Bad Ones.

New York: Random House Business.

Duhigg, Charles. (2014).,

The Power of Habit: Why We Do What We Do in Life and Business.

New York: Random House.

Ellis, Albert. (1998).,

Rational Emotive Behavior Therapy: A Therepist's Guide

California: IMPACT Publishers.

Knight, Sue. (2002).,

NLP at Work: The Essence of Excellence.

London: Nicholas Brealey Publishers.

Kolb, David, A. (2014).,

Experiential Learning: Experience as the Source of Learning and Development.

New Jersey: Pearson FT Press.

Lindsey Agness. (2010).,

Change Your Life with NLP: The Powerful Way to Make Your Whole Life Bette.

London: Ft Press.

Miltenberger, R.G. (2015).,

Behavior Modification: Principles and Procedures.

California: Wadsworth Publishing Co.

Renuka Raj Sing et. al. (2022).,

T-Group Facilitation: Theory and Practice of Applied Behavioural Science.

London: Taylor and Francis Ltd.

Tuman, M.F. (2020).,

Sensitivity Training: Blue Has No Feelings.

Chicago: Independent Publishing.

Subject Index